W9-BRD-435

# THE NEW
# FREEDOM
## OF
# FORGIVENESS

# THE NEW
# FREEDOM
## OF
# FORGIVENESS

## DAVID AUGSBURGER

**MOODY PRESS**
CHICAGO

Third Edition © 2000 by
DAVID AUGSBURGER

Copyright 1970,1988 by
MOODY BIBLE INSTITUTE

Original title (1970): *Seventy Times Seven*
Second Edition (1988): *The Freedom of Forgiveness*

Study Guide
© 2000 by
JAMES S. BELL JR.

All rights reserved. No part of this book may be reproduced in any form without permission in writing from the publisher, except in the case of brief quotations embodied in critical articles or reviews.

Scripture quotations, unless noted otherwise, are from J. B. Phillips's *The New Testament in Modern English,* © J. B. Phillips, 1958, published by the Macmillan Company, New York City.

Scripture quotations marked (NIV) are taken from the *Holy Bible: New International Version®.* NIV®. Copyright © 1973, 1978, 1984 by International Bible Society. Used by permission of Zondervan Publishing House. All rights reserved.

Scripture quotations marked (NEB) are taken from the *New English Bible* © 1961, 1970 by the Delegates of the Oxford University Press and the Syndics of the Cambridge University Press.

Scripture quotations marked (KJV) are taken from the King James Version.

The use of selected references from various versions of the Bible in this publication does not necessarily imply publisher endorsement of the versions in their entirety.

Library of Congress Cataloging-in-Publication Data

Augsburger, David W.
    The new freedom of forgiveness / by David Augsburger.--3rd ed.
        p.cm.
    Rev. ed. of Freedom of forgiveness. 1988.
    Includes bibliographical references.
    ISBN 0-8024-3292-1 (pbk.)
        1. Forgiveness--Religious aspects--Christianity. I. Augsburger, David W. Freedom of forgiveness. II. Title.

BV4647.F55 A94 2000
234'.5--dc21

99-086117

5 7 9 10 8 6 4

*Printed in the United States of America*

To
Those many, many persons,
Who, like their Galilean Teacher,
Forgive
   And forgive
   And forgive
   And forgive
Without waiting
   for memory fatigue,
Without resorting
   to pious denial,
Without substituting
   empty tolerance,
But forgive
And forgive again.

# CONTENTS

# PREFACE TO THE
# THIRD EDITION

Forgiveness must be one of the deepest human hungers.

Why else would this little book go on passing from hand to hand, being given and received as a gift or used in study groups, year after year?

Perhaps because we find it necessary to ask the hard questions about forgiving repeatedly in our daily relationships; perhaps because it doesn't get any easier the second, third, or thirty-third time; perhaps because we discover it is not something we are able to do for others as much as it is something we at last discover we too need and must find if we are to live with those about us.

At the encouragement of readers, counselors, and pastors who have used it to support reconciliation, the book has been rewritten, strengthened, illustrated with further stories from life, and sharpened in its focus on what true forgiveness is about—the regaining of a sister or brother. In Jesus' words, that is the goal of faithful forgiving —not the personal release of letting go and healing yourself or finding healing for yourself, but the reconstruction and transformation of relationships.

Forgiveness is something we discover, more than something we do; it is something we gratefully receive, more than something we faithfully give. Perhaps in reading these words on forgiving, you will find the hope of forgiving someone who has done you wrong becoming more clear, the courage to seek forgiveness from someone you have injured more strong, and, at last, the experience of forgiveness, painful as it is, more precious.

# PREFACE TO THE
# FIRST EDITION

Forgiveness is costly.

Outrageously costly. *Seventy Times Seven* [the original title of this book] explores a few of the four hundred eighty-nine varieties of hurt where healing can only come from complete forgiveness. The forgiveness that frees both forgiver and forgiven.

Portions of the material in these chapters appeared first as radio messages on the "Mennonite Hour" broadcast. Wherever possible, quotations have been credited, but many conscious and unconscious references to the writing of others are beyond identification.

Special appreciation goes to James G. T. Fairfield, for his editorial and critical assistance.

And thanks to God for the many people who have shown me in life how to accept the cost of forgiving.

# 1

# WHY SEEK FORGIVENESS?

Once upon a time, as all good stories begin, a Mennonite farmer bequeathed his farm to his two sons. At first they worked the land together, sharing labor, splitting the profits. As time passed, they married, built separate homes, raised sons and daughters of their own, divided the land, and ran neighboring farms. Sadly, they grew apart, rarely spoke. Then one took offense, the other was outraged, and a bitter quarrel ensued.

One morning the older brother rose to see that a lake had appeared overnight in what had been the meadow between their homes. His brother's bulldozer sat where a great rock pile once stood. Now the rocks formed a curved wall that turned a meandering stream into a rising flood.

"Well, I'll be!" he said. "Then I'll go him one better. I'm calling the nursery and ordering a dozen twelve-foot pine trees to block his view." The day after the trees went in, the younger brother installed shutters to seal off his windows. The older brother angrily countered by moving six hog houses and a hundred sows and shoats upwind of his brother's house . . . who replied by cutting off the water pipeline to their common spring, which was on the side of his hill.

So the older brother went for the throat. The old wooden bridge on their shared private road would have to go. This would force his brother to take a long detour to the main road. He called for a wrecker to drop the bridge and a load of lumber to erect safety barriers.

The next morning he met the young carpenter that was sent out, gave him his orders, and withdrew to await the next move. That evening he went down to survey the wreckage. As he rounded the hill, there stood a newly rebuilt bridge—wider, more beautiful, with craftsman railings. And his brother stood in the middle, marveling at the workmanship. He turned and came toward him with outstretched hand.

"I can't believe you'd do this for us, after all I've said and done to you. It takes a big man to take the first step. I'm sorry for my behavior." They seized each other's hands, then turned to see the carpenter swinging into his pickup.

"Hey, wait," they both shouted to him, "not so fast. Please stay; we've got a lot of rebuilding to do around here."

"I can see that you do," he replied, "but how can I do anything else when there are so many bridges to build?"

❧   ❧   ❧

Forgiveness, the interpersonal bridge that reconnects alienated sisters and brothers, friends, and enemies is so difficult to build. Is it truly possible? Can anyone actually forgive, or is "forgiveness" a special kind of denial that allows us to pretend that all is well again? Or perhaps it is a kind of memory fatigue that overwhelms our anger when we grow exhausted with resenting? Or is it a divine gift that allows us to finish the past and reopen the future? Is it a one-way action of ending the hot hostilities or calling off the cold war? Or does it take two to do that deep kind of reconciling called *forgiving* in the biblical story?

The more familiar stories of forgiveness are not two-way. They tend to be the individual stories of one person finding the mystery of a forgiving heart while the other person in the drama goes another way. The following story offers such a pattern of unilateral lonely movement from rage to a new beginning. Consider its deeper meaning to explore the alternate story of finding healing, which is the second of these two poles that form these contrasting understandings of forgiveness.

## Betrayal and Bitterness

"This is it. I'm calling it quits with her! I've had it." Having said it aloud to the barren desert, the man—lean, with that stringiness of muscle and etching of face that tell of hard work and time's abrasion —stood up from his rocky seat and began picking his way down the butte to the ranch. A long night—in fact, a whole decade—of wrestling with anger lay behind him. Now he would wash his hands of his wife in the quietest way he could.

It had all begun so differently. The tenderness of courtship, those first expressions of love, the excitement when a little daughter was born, then their two sons. The ranch was building itself into security; friendships were knit into the fabric of community. Their shared faith and life in God lay beneath it all.

Then—the first night when she wouldn't talk. So unlike her! The children chatted as usual; she smiled. But something gray and impenetrable, some distance that could never be crossed, had appeared between them. Her quietness stretched across months. It became too painful, so they turned for help. First to their minister, but nothing cracked the shell of silence. Then to their doctor, but nothing seemed clear. To a psychiatrist, but nothing opened communication.

Years passed, years in which the silent coexistence slowly embittered their daughter, driving her to a job in the East. The scars began to appear in the other children. He spent all the time he could with them, trying to make up for it all.

Then she found a new friend to lean on—a liquid friend. At times, the alcohol made things easier as she passed through the talkative stage and her words would begin a tentative response to the love and acceptance he'd given her through the bitter years.

One night, when she'd had a drop too much, she began to talk. Once started, there seemed no stopping. A wistful memory of happy recollections of those first years together. Then she froze in silence, groping for some opening, some crack in the wall of years past. Then, at last, the story surfaced.

There was a man who used to come by the ranch routinely in his work. He'd stop by the house too. For her, it was a friendly break in the lonesome daytime hours with the kids at school. For him, it soon became more. For a while, she laughed at his advances; but they grew on her, until in a moment of unexpected passion began the long relationship. Years of festered fear and guilt spilled as she told it. "You will never know who it was," she said, "Anyway, it's the last person you'd ever suspect."

"Who was it?" he demanded, feeling hatred begin to churn in his viscera. For ten years he had accepted it all; but now, knowing that his worst fears were true, that a betrayal had taken place, he could not stop the spread of anger through him. Day after day he prodded, until he got the name. His oldest, though not best friend. A man he'd trusted implicitly, one who had everything he himself had wished for his own family life. Something soured and died within him.

"I'll get him; I'll get him," he said again and again. "I'll burn him in front of his wife. She's a proud one. She'll rub him in the dirt until he's face-to-face with another worm."

All that night he had wandered bitter-blind over familiar trails. Now hot with rage, now chilled with hate. Morning found him frozen with revenge. And it was Sunday.

"Why I went to church that morning I'll never know," he told me later. "Something in me I could not hear must have been crying for help. I stepped through the door, and there he stood, hand out, the same old smile.

"My hand froze to my pocket. I struggled for what may have been seconds. To me it was eternity.

"'I'll never forgive that man,' I'd vowed again and again. 'He'll pay for every painful moment I've suffered through ten miserable years.'

"But now, a heart full of hatred fought with a truth that broke over me as I faced the enemy.

"That truth I'd prayed automatically since childhood, 'Forgive me my debts just as I forgive my debtors.' And the echoing warning, 'If you will not forgive, neither will your heavenly Father forgive your failures.'

"Then, somehow, I took the hand of the man who'd betrayed everything I loved. I began to understand how brutally hard it is to forgive. Slowly the residues of bitterness begin to drain out of me, and I found the first signs of courage to try again. It would not be easy to find a way through the massive barrier separating me from my wife. If, someday, we could say to each other, 'I accept you just as I did that day we pledged to love and cherish until death,' then healing could work its slow change.

"I thought I could never forgive, but I suspect that no matter what has been done against you, no matter what hurt has been inflicted, forgiveness is possible."

❧    ❧    ❧

This is a story of courage, of the slow discovery of a forgiving heart, of one man's journey toward opening the soul, but is it a story of forgiveness? It is focused on the inner battle between rage at injustice and the realization that both parties are in need of healing. It says little about the pain of the wife, the suffering of the children, the blindness of the friend/enemy. It speaks only of the private inner movement of the betrayed.

Is this forgiveness? In the common language of Western culture, of common Christian piety, of most evangelical teaching, this is the heart of forgiveness. But in the teaching of Jesus, this is only the first step. It is the "restoring perceptions" step of the respect we call "love of neighbor" or "love of the enemy." Both of these are the base of all forgiving, but they are not forgiveness. To forgive, one must go beyond the recognition that the other who has wronged you is a fellow human being who is of worth and value (the step that leads to restoring love for the other). That step beyond is the crucial step Christ called "forgiving." It is a step that offers or invites repentance and that risks or trusts the self in restoring or reconstructing the central relationship and all the interconnected relationships that form the interlocking web of the story.

But before we can explore what it is that we truly mean by forgiving, how far we need to go, and what steps we might take, we must ask the prior question: Why would anyone seek to forgive when resentment feels so good, when anger seems so justified, and when healing would cost so much? That is the prior question. Why try? Why seek it at the outset? Why not take the safer paths of flight or fight?

## Why Should One Forgive?

When the injury is so painful, who can avoid asking, Why should I forgive? What's the point? Why shouldn't the person who has wronged me be made to pay for his or her sins? Why shouldn't he be punished? Why shouldn't she suffer?

If any conviction about such things comes naturally, it's the deep-seated belief that "somebody's got to pay." Forgiveness seems too easy. There should be blood for blood. Eye for eye.

If it's a tooth in question, one can require tooth for tooth in retaliation. But what repayment can anyone demand from the man who has broken your home or betrayed your daughter? What can you ask from the woman who has ruined your reputation? So few sins can be paid for, and so seldom does the victim possess the power or the advantage to demand payment. In most cases, "making things right" is beyond possibility. How can you get back what another has taken from you emotionally, socially, relationally?

Repayment is impossible! (Although at first flush, it is desirable.)

What then of revenge? If you cannot get equal payment or restitution from the offender, at least you can get vengeance. If the one who wronged you cannot repay you, perhaps you can pay him back in kind, tit for tat. Serve the same sauce. Now "an eye for an eye" takes on new meaning.

But here, too, there is an intrinsic and insurmountable problem— as you try to get even, you actually become even with your enemy. You bring yourself to the same level, and below. There is a saying that goes, "Doing an injury puts you below your enemy; revenging an injury makes you but even; only forgiving sets you above."

Revenge not only lowers you to your enemy's lowest level; what's worse, it boomerangs; it continues the injury within you. Revenge is not its own reward; it is its own *punishment*. In effect, it aims the weapon of revenge at oneself in hope of hurting the enemy with the kick of the gun's recoil. Then it shoots the self in the foot—you have no moral leg to stand on—and it reloads and shoots the other foot in cyclical resentment. It spites the self in sustaining spiteful feelings toward the other. Revenge is a worthless weapon. It corrupts the avenger while continuing the enemy's wrongdoing. It initiates an endless flight down the bottomless stairway of rancor, reprisals, and ruthless retaliation. It accepts the foe's terms, tactics, and treachery and blindly repeats it.

Just as repayment is impossible, revenge is impotent! (Although it wears the mask of power.)

No repayment? No revenge? But what of the soul-satisfaction of resentment? In its raw form, resentment takes the soul hostage, holds itself captive to the offender, binds the bitter heart to the oppressor. Nursing a grudge until it grows into a full-blown hate—

hoofs, horns, tail, and all—offers a sort of stubborn self-comfort, but when hatred is harbored, it grows, spreads, and contaminates all other emotions. Ultimately, hatred is the costliest of companions. The warmth it provides fuels deeper fires that sear the soul on both conscious and unconscious levels.

Hidden hatred turns trust into suspicion, compassion into caustic criticism, and faith in others into cold cynicism. Incubated hatred can elevate blood pressure, ulcerate a stomach, accelerate stress, or invite a coronary.

Hatred—the wish for another's destruction—is self-destructive. It is more prudent to pardon than to resent. The exorbitant cost of anger, the extravagant expense of hatred, and the unreasonable interest we pay on grudges make resentment a questionable pleasure at the least and a costly compulsion at the best, or worst. It is wisest to deal with hatred before the sting swells, before a molehill mushrooms into a mountain, before a spark kindles conflagration.

What a strange thing bitterness is! It boils up within us when we need it least, when we're down and in desperate need of all our freedom, ability, and energy to get back up. And what strange things bitterness can do to us. Like a permanent plaster cast, it slowly sets, perhaps protecting us from further pain but ultimately holding us rigid in frozen animation or rigor mortis. Feelings turn to stone; responses become concrete. Bitterness is paralysis. Parts of the personality no longer respond to signals from the soul.

A young man falsely accused and penalized by his high school principal turns sullen, angry, and bitter. His faith in justice and authority dies. He may wait years to begin to thaw.

A girl betrayed by a guy she trusted is forced, becomes pregnant, then turns bitter and withdrawn. Her faith in humanity ends. She may need a lifetime to come to terms with the evil done.

A woman deserted by her husband and left to be both mother and father to their two sons turns angry at life—at the whole universe. Her faith in God and everything good has ended. She cannot live long enough to let the fire burn out on its own.

Bitterness is such a potent paralyzer of mind, soul, and spirit that it can freeze reason and emotion. Our attitudes turn cynical, uncaring, critical, and caustic. Where we once ventured to place faith in others, now we trust no one. Turtlelike, we withdraw inside protective shells of distrust, burned once, twice shy.

Letting bitterness seal us in can be an excuse for acting irresponsibly. Being responsible in any painful situation usually calls for us to accept our part of the blame for the way things are. But being bitter about it can save us all that. We can scapegoat others. We may feel fully justified in blaming God for our troubles and difficulties.

Bitterness is a cyclical, repetitive, tightly closed circle of self-centered pain. It carries us around and around a senseless arc—around and around ourselves. Like a child learning to ride a bicycle, knowing how to ride but not how to stop, we pedal on and on, afraid to quit, yet wishing for someone to grab the bars, stop our circling, and let us off. Bitterness is useless. Repayment is impossible. Revenge is impotent. Resentment is impractical.

## What Is This Forgiveness We Are Seeking?

When the forgiveness we understand is a private process of inner healing, not an interpersonal bridge that can stretch across the empty void between two injured persons to reconcile differences and restore relationships, it feeds and fosters acts of resentment, revenge, retaliation, or demanding repayment Since these are not possible or practical, the solution is to cut off the connection with the offender, with the community that permitted or ignores the offense, and with all those who appear to be complicit in the offense. Rejecting all relationships that have failed us is the most common "solution" in our contemporary Western culture, among Christians and non-Christians alike. Cut off the old connections, withdraw from all interaction, live at a distance, avoid intimacy or involvement. Above all, do not risk working at forgiveness.

As common as this option is, it is destructive of human relationships, fragments personality, and it is inconsistent with the basic values of any faith commitment.

Only if you have no need of forgiveness yourself do you dare consider hesitating to forgive another. The two go hand in hand. Jesus linked these as two aspects of the one and same reality. "If you forgive other people their failures, your Heavenly Father will also forgive you. But if you will not forgive . . . , neither will your Heavenly Father forgive you your failures" (Matthew 6:14–15).

"I never forgive," General James Oglethorpe, the governor of Georgia, said to the young John Wesley.

"Then I hope, sir," replied Wesley, "that you never sin!"

George Herbert, the English poet, hymnist, and pastor once wrote, "One who cannot forgive others breaks the bridge over which all must pass if they would ever reach heaven; for everyone has need to be forgiven." Forgiving and being forgiven are all of one piece; in giving we receive, accepting those who have injured us we open ourselves to God's acceptance. There is no sequence of time or priority. The two are one. Anyone who loves God shows it in neighbor-love. The rush of God's strength, which brings forgiveness, gives in turn the ability to forgive—and forgive again. Paradoxically, the two are not two but one. Contradictory as this sounds in proposition, it is clear when seen in story. A story Jesus told is the perfect paradigm (see Matthew 18:21–35).

A certain poor man owed his king $2 million. He couldn't pay, so the king ordered the man, his wife, his children, and his property sold to pay the debt. The man, face in the dust, pleaded with the king, "Oh, sir, be patient! I'll pay it all."

"Two million dollars? Impossible!" said the king. But then, in pity, he forgave him all his debt.

The man, overjoyed, left the king. Outside he met a neighbor who owed him twenty dollars.

"Pay up," he demanded.

"Just be patient, and I'll have it for you next week."

"Nothing doing," said the man, and had him thrown into the debtors' prison.

The king got wind of it all and summoned the man. "You evil wretch," he said, "here I canceled that tremendous debt for you, and you have the collosal gall to be unforgiving of a few dollars. You have sentenced yourself! Jail until you pay $2 million."

Then said Jesus to His listeners, "God can do no other unless each of you forgives your brother from the heart."

# 2

# WHAT THEN
# IS FORGIVENESS?

I had a brother once, and I betrayed him."

With these words, African writer Laurens Van der Post begins a profound human drama in his book *The Seed and the Sower* (New York: Morrow, 1963).

Two brothers grew up in a small South African village. The older was tall, handsome, intelligent, an excellent athlete, a good student, and a natural leader. Sent away to a private school, he quickly made a name for himself. As an admired campus leader, brilliant student, and outstanding athlete, he was in his final year when his younger brother arrived to begin studies.

The little brother was not good-looking or athletic. He was a hunchback. Since his childhood his mother had sewn padded jackets that concealed his spinal deformity. His sensitivity to his short, curved stature had grown through the years. None of the family spoke of it out of respect for his shamed feelings. Yet the boy had one great gift. He had a magnificent voice and could sing gloriously, like a nightingale on the veldt.

Soon after his arrival at the private school, the students held initiation ceremonials that included hazing—a sort of trial by fire—a public humiliation to extract proof of courage. Often one student would be singled out to be especially hounded as a kind of scapegoat. On the eve of the initiation, the student body in a cruel mob action ganged up on the younger brother, carried him off to the water tank, and demanded that the acclaimed singer sing while they jeered. His fear only focused the purity of his tenor and the frighteningly beautiful sound only incited the crowd to be all the more abusive. Finally, they tore off his padded shirt to reveal his never-before-seen hunchback.

The older brother, aware of what was planned, watched silently from the laboratory window. He could have stepped through the playful mob turned sadistic and with a word put a stop to the whole tragic scene. As a leader, he could have acknowledged the strange boy as his brother, but instead he busied himself in his work in the laboratory while the mob raged outside. By refusing to go to him in love when he was being abused, he betrayed his brother.

The younger brother never sang again. He survived physically, but his spirit was crushed. He withdrew into himself. At the end of the term he returned to the family farm, where he lived a lonely, reclusive life.

The older brother rose to prominence in the capital and when World War II came was commissioned as an officer and posted in Palestine. One night, recovering from an injury, he lay under the stars in restless sleep and troubled dreams. As in a vision, he saw himself in the gathering of disciples. Christ Jesus surveyed the circle and protested, "Someone is missing; it is Judas."

"Where is Judas my brother?"

The dreamer spoke. "I am Judas; I had a brother once, and I betrayed him."

"Go to your brother," Christ replied.

The journey from Palestine was exhausting for the recovering man. He arrived unannounced, was given a cold welcome by his brother's wife, and at last found his brother watering plants in the parched garden, seeking to save his young trees in a time of long drought.

His brother's silence spoke of a soul still imprisoned in the painful past. That moment of tortured time arrested was visible in face as well as form.

"I've come all this distance on a weekend leave to spend a few hours with you," the older brother said, then went straight to the matter of his great wrong. When he had finished, both were in tears, yet silent in their pain. The first rainstorm of the year was breaking as the older brother walked back to the house and the younger turned off the irrigation water.

Then in the distance the elder brother heard the song of his brother in the garden, as he had not heard him sing since childhood. A song of his own writing in boyhood, but now with a new verse.

> I rode all through the night
> To the fire in the distance burning
> And beside the fire found
> He who had waited for so long.

## Regaining the Other as Sister or Brother

Van der Post understood Jesus. A novelist got it right where theologians and counselors often go astray by forgetting the heart of it all—regaining the brother—and instead get caught up in pursuing cultural values of individualism, self-actualization, self-emancipation, and self-healing. His story is a commentary on the combined texts of Matthew 5:23–24 and 18:15–20.

"Go to your brother," said Jesus, "and if he will hear you, you have regained your brother." For Jesus, this is the goal—the central focus, the true meaning of forgiveness. The primary issue is not inner peace for oneself, not moral rightness with one's own conscience, not assurance of one's own salvation. These are self-centered, narcissistic goals that are only further evidence of the fact that one is still giving primary care to one's own needs and secondary—if any—care to the relationship or to the pain in the other.

In the modern Western world, writing on forgiveness is almost exclusively focused on the process within, the virtues of the freedom found by the forgiver. It is common for teaching on forgiveness never to get to what Jesus actually taught, but to focus only on tolerance and love. Important as these are, they are but the first steps toward forgiveness. Before forgiveness can be sought, one must risk taking the prerequisite steps of (left foot) seeing the other person as having worth again and (right foot) restoring perceptions of love. Then comes the long leap toward forgiving.

Unfortunately, most writing on forgiveness in Western Chris-

tianity speaks only of this first movement from rejection to acceptance, from angry brooding to release and inner peace. One cannot
help noting that in much good literature on the subject, one could
omit the word *forgiveness* and speak only of *love,* since, in New Testament terms, the choice to love the other again is all that is addressed.
But if being able to love the offender or the offended once more were
all that was needed, then both parties could take the step of attitudinal change in the privacy of their own homes or the hidden cham-
bers of the heart. They could go forward in life without a deeper
conversation about repentance, change, and reconstructing the relationship.

But that is not what Jesus intended. "If your brother has a grievance against you, *go to him*" (Matthew 5:23–24, paraphrase). "If you
have something against your brother, *go to him*" (Matthew 18:15, paraphrase). "If your brother sins, *confront him*" (Luke 17:3, paraphrase).

These are Jesus' central words on working through injury and
working out forgiveness. They do not describe desirable *consequences*
of forgiveness as we commonly hear taught but the central and unavoidable *process.* We are not engaged in the process of forgiving and
being forgiven until we seek to take whatever steps are possible toward attempting to restore, reconstruct, and rediscover a relationship. Such steps may be limited by the other's death, distance,
emotional cutoff, refusal to converse, or disappearance from the community. But seeking forgiveness is not an optional goal. It is the *central task,* and when it is not possible we grieve, feel the loss, experience
the failure of the relationship, talk about it with a surrogate, and search
our own hearts to offer our deep willingness to reach out for reconciliation.

## What Is Forgiving?

"*Forgiveness* is not a proper English word, so do not use it," I once
heard Kenneth Cragg, the great Christian-Islamic scholar say. "You
don't add *ness* to a verb to make a noun. Instead, you add it to an
adjective to turn it into a noun—like goodness, badness, niceness,
rudeness. But you cannot create a word like forgiveness. So whenever
you use it you must remember that it must have an apostrophe. The
true word is either *forgivenness* or *forgivingness* but definitely not forgiveness. Perhaps there's a message there," he added, "A sermon per-

haps, because only when you have experienced forgivenness can you truly express forgivingness."

Perhaps a further reason we should give up the word is because it has come to mean so many things to so many people that its central significance is not only confused, but largely lost. In popular usage in Western individualistic cultures, *forgiveness* has become a word for accepting reality, admitting our failures and finitude, facing self-defeating behavior, becoming able to manage time properly by separating past and present so that the one does not flood into the other, or of taking control of one's own side of any painful relationship. Here is a collected listing of contemporary definitions of *forgiveness*, a sort of reconciliation wish list—or wash list.

*Forgiveness is something you do for yourself, not for the other.* It is not for the one who hurt you; it is an act done for your own good. You free yourself from the continuation of the pain and the review of anger. You do this because you deserve the healing, no matter what the other deserves.

*Forgiveness is self-emancipation.* It is a way of releasing oneself from the pain suffered at the hands of another. It is putting an end to blaming oneself for being a victim or a participant in the hurt and is a refusal to continue to blame the other. It is a cessation of judgment—of judging self or the other.

*Forgiveness is taking ownership; it is taking control.* The purpose of forgiveness is to reclaim control of your own life by letting go of unpleasant events and people, moving free from the injury, and turning toward the future. You evict the other from occupying your mind—rent-free—and usurping your mental world; you refuse to be held emotional hostage by him.

*Forgiveness is in your power to choose, to act, to leap ahead.* It is a power each of us possesses independently of the other's attitudes or actions. It is a courageous choice, a decisive act, a wise option, a noble move away from old entrapment to new freedom.

*Forgiveness is a refusal to condone evil or to accept injustice as inevitable, tolerable, or explainable.* It does not imply that you agree in any way with what the other did, how he defended himself, or what he believes about the painful event or act. It is simply your recognition that the past is past. You cannot erase the act or change the deed. But you can leave it in the past and move forward toward freedom.

*Forgiveness releases us from self-absorption and self-destruction.* Hold-

ing on to anger hurts the anger bearer, not the target. It slowly dam-
ages the soul of the irritated, not the irritant. By not forgiving the
wrongdoer, but instead reviewing and renewing the wrongdoing daily, we extend the pain. By nailing the other to his past, we nail ourselves to our own. Thou shalt not nail another to his past. Why should
you nail yourself to your own?

*Forgiveness allows us to give up suffering.* The need to suffer is mis-
directed aggression; the need to be pitied is passive aggression; the
need to be right is self-justification and perfectionism supported by
other-blame. All of these serve to keep us connected to the perpetrator through rage.

*Forgiveness is more powerful than anger.* Anger is a reaction to feelings of impotence; it is an attempt to grasp the power we have lost.
Forgiveness, though it may appear weak, is actually strong—it takes
a powerful position of change, defines the self anew, and refuses to
be dominated and overwhelmed by another's evil acts. It ends our ob-
session with feeling vulnerable and then protecting ourselves by re-
cycling and refueling our anger helplessly.

*Forgiveness is positive detachment, constructive distancing.* One cuts
off the connection to the pain event; severs the pain nerve linking the
soul to the injury; distances the self from the negative memory; ceas-
es to define the self as a victim; and detaches the self from the pain
cluster of old thoughts, ruminations, broodings, and grudges.

*Forgiveness is a private ritual of release.* It is *attunement* where there
is no *atonement.* You must enact an inner ritual of personal cleansing
that ejects the blocks that keep you stuck, evicts the monsters you use
to represent the other, cancels your demands and expectations con-
cerning how he should act toward you, and chooses to let go. You
burn your lists of grievances. You visualize the other as moving toward the light in his own twisting or twisted path. You realize that if
reconciliation is to happen, it will come at some future time as a
gift. There is nothing you can do to force it, so be at peace without
it.

Are these appropriate definitions of forgiving? Certainly they
are full of truth about coming to terms with reality and accepting our
own humanity, frailty, and need for humility. Indeed, they offer wisdom about letting go of our pretensions of controlling the other or
of being in control of the relationship. True, they are helpful in rewrit-
ing our inner self-instructions (the self-talk that goes on and on in

our minds when we review an injury.) Yes, they are helpful in moving toward healing through relinquishment. All these are necessary.

But is this forgiveness in any historic biblical, theological, and genuinely relational definition? After appreciating the way the list helps us to turn away from grandiose fantasies of taking control of the other, the situation, and the final outcome, we are left with the recognition that this list is a description, not of forgiveness, but of the *prerequisite* to all forgiving—of recognizing one's own powerlessness to change others, releasing fantasies of omnipotence, and turning from rage to explore the possibilities of seeing the other again as a fellow human being who is precious in spite of what he has done against us. This is a necessary step. This is important work. This is the groundwork of restoring attitudes of love on which forgiveness will stand if it is to ever happen. But forgiving is risking something more.

*Forgiving is risking a return to conversation and a resumption of relationship.* Forgiveness in the New Testament sense is more synonymous with our understanding of *reconciliation* than with *love.* The two Greek words for forgiveness are translated most clearly as "to release or set free" and "to offer a gift of grace."

Word studies done on these words apart from context, usage, story, and setting allow Western individualists to define forgiveness as a private releasing of another, a personal gift of grace within the believer's heart. But in the scriptural context, the meaning is always relational; it is addressing the actual interactions between offended people. We are called to "forgive as God in Christ has forgiven" (Colossians 3:13, paraphrased from the KJV; cf. Ephesians 4:32)—and that is not a detached private pardon or release. God's forgiveness in Jesus was utterly, totally invested in incarnational involvement, crucified self-commitment, and life-blood contact with us humans. There is no cheap forgiveness in Christ, who is our example, model, and empowerment.

## The Painful Journey

Forgiving is not an immediate solution, an attitudinal change of instant release, or a quick fix. Instead, it is a painful journey, an extended wrestling with the injury, a *process*—brief and deep or long and difficult—which has its own stations (like the road to the Cross) of Gethsemane, trial, suffering, and sometimes a bit of the Cross. If all forgiveness, whether human or divine, proceeds from the same paradigm, as the apostle Paul repeatedly insists it does, then it should come as no surprise that forgiveness is an inestimably costly task for God and for those made in God's image. The Cross shows how demanding it was for God to forgive, how far God was willing to go to forgive, and how costly it is to forgive.

The English poet, novelist, and dramatist Dorothy Sayers describes it well:

> *Hard it is, very hard,*
> *To travel up the slow and stony road*
> *To Calvary, to redeem mankind; far better*
> *To make but one resplendent miracle,*
> *Lean through the cloud, lift the right hand of power*
> *And with a sudden lightning smite the world perfect.*
> *Yet this was not God's way, Who had the power,*
> *But set it by, choosing the cross, the thorn,*
> *The sorrowful wounds. Something there is, perhaps,*
> *That power destroys in passing, something supreme,*
> *To whose great value in the eyes of God*
> *That cross, that thorn, and those five wounds bear witness.*[1]

Why does serious talk about forgiveness require us to talk about God on a cross? Because God accepted the Cross to make forgiveness possible and to model forgiving to an unforgiving world.

*The Christ of the Cross is our great example.* "Christ suffered for you, leaving you an example, that you should follow in his steps," wrote the apostle Peter (1 Peter 2:21 NIV).

In Jesus we see compassionate forgiving modeled. We see forgiving love embodied. We see faithfulness to truth in relationships carried to its authentic conclusion. We see human possibilities that we are called to own and experience. We see the face of God, and it is a face of forgiving love.

That face offers us the ultimate example to live by, and the love shining from that face offers us the power to live in new ways. Just as admiring beauty will not make us beautiful, so respecting an example of goodness will not improve our character. All lasting change comes within relationships—and the final relationship that can set us free is encountering this God; knowing God at whatever level we are mature enough to experience; and yearning to incorporate—

not just imitate—His example, to truly become and be like Him. This transforming relationship is at the heart of forgiveness.

For centuries, this internal attraction that transforms motivation—the inner urge to return to the one who hurt you in seeking forgiveness—has been called the "moral influence of the cross." All moral decisions are altered since the event on Calvary. Jesus Himself said, "I, if I be lifted up . . . , will draw all men unto me" (John 12:32 KJV). Christ's self-sacrifice was not just a "great example." It was utterly unparalleled self-sacrifice done in total faithfulness to virtue and offered in undeniable courage so as to be completely true to His vision and calling. It was suffered in such scalding humility that it makes us thoroughly ashamed of ourselves and our self-centered living. It is a display of such unlimited love that it makes us sick of our unloving inhumanity to one another. It is the kind of compassion that shows us up as the sinners we are and breaks up our rebellious spirit. The moral influence of His act changes our attitude toward God. In gratitude we live for Him. His virtuous life and deeds were carried in relationships with others that modeled deep reconciliation and forgiveness.

Yet there is much more. Jesus was not just a fantastically good and righteous folk hero who died nobly, unjustly, and tragically to show us the highest good. His death had a greater, more personal effect on our lives. It is relationally connected to our inner ledgers of guilt, shame, and anxiety before God and others.

*The Christ of the Cross is God's final word, not just of love, but of justice.* There is a baseline of justice; and God is a God of faithful, radical fairness and redemptive justice who loves that which is the good. God cannot either permissively or explicitly overlook human inhumanity, murder, rebellion, selfishness, and all the rest of the evil we do and are. God, the first of all integers, is Integrity, and He deals with evil with no evasion.

God became human—a divine Human—in Jesus Christ to stand with us in our evil, to bear with us and for us the inevitable and inescapable consequence for what we have done and do in choosing to be what we all are—sinners! "At just the right time, when we were still powerless, Christ died for the ungodly" (Romans 5:6 NIV). "He himself bore our sins in his body on the tree" (1 Peter 2:24 NIV). Our Forgiver and our forgiveness, Jesus Christ became our Reconciliation. He reconnects us to God and to each other, and through this transformation to our true nature—our true selves. "God was in Christ personally reconciling the world to himself" (2 Corinthians 5:19).

This was no scapegoating! This isn't an ugly story of God's punishing Jesus for our sins. Morally and justly the guilt of one's sins cannot be transferred to a third party. It must be settled between the two involved.

Either the sinner bears his own guilt (that's cold justice); or the one sinned against, the first party, may absorb what the second party did (that's sacrifice); or the two may meet in transforming repentance and redemption (that's forgiveness). And that's what God did in Christ at Calvary. He "[tasted] death for everyone" (Hebrews 2:9 NIV) in sacrifice; He identified with us in incarnation, life, ministry, and in His ongoing life in the church. He has fully encountered humankind in forgiving love as well as forgiving integrity. "Grace and truth" came to "[us] by Jesus Christ" (John 1:17 KJV). Gracious acceptance blended with truthful confrontation invites healing and growth. Both are essential in working through to true forgiveness.

Authentic forgiveness is the mutual recognition that repentance is genuine and right relationships are achieved. Forgiving requires the *grace* to accept the other as an equal partner in the search for reconciliation and the *genuineness* to give repentance—or to respond to another's repentance—with full trust and respect. Grace and truth, acceptance and confrontation, sacrifice and prophetic rebuke are needed in resolving alienation, injustice, or interpersonal injuries.

In forgiveness we go to the sister; we seek out the brother; we rediscover each other. That is the goal of forgiveness. It was God's way with us; it must be our way with each other. We are to forgive one another as God in Christ has forgiven us. Forgiveness is not finally complete until the severed friendship is mended. And the new weld of forgiveness should afterward result in a deeper, stronger union than existed before!

The final step in forgiving is reconnecting with the one who has hurt you and discovering that the link that comes in the strange chemistry of reconciliation can heal the wound until nothing remains but the remembered scar. And even its meaning is changed in the remembering.

⤻    ⤻    ⤻

In the early 1980s, in Southern California, a young girl was abducted, molested, and murdered. The murderer was arrested, convicted, and sentenced to life in prison, but this legal process brought no healing or consolation to the mother. Unable to shake the rage that flooded her each day, she quit her job and, with her family, moved to a new location to start again. Then she moved again, and then again. Nothing changed except for the deepening of the pain.

One day a new acquaintance invited her to go along to church. Her response was indifferent, but the friend persisted, and gradually something triggered the beginning of a journey of change. In part, it was the warmth of the circle of new friends, then the support of a prayer group, then the beginnings of exploring the Bible. Slowly, painfully, over a period of three to four years, she discovered that the memories of her daughter were taking on a different color and tone. The recollections of happy days with her daughter began to offer peace rather than remorse and resentment. Forgotten memories appeared to awaken gratitude and surprising joy in recalling her daughter's life. And her feelings toward the murderer began to grow less cold as the monster began to take on human dimensions. In astonishment, she heard herself, as from a distance, use words about forgiving what had been eternally outside any consideration of forgiveness. She began to talk about this with friends, in a small group, and once in a church service.

Once the transformation began, it accelerated as she accepted an invitation to talk to parents of murdered children, then to several groups of prisoners. Through a chaplain of a nearby state penitentiary she was invited to share her experience in a prison chapel service. She clung to the pulpit as her story of years of torment and slow, inexplicable recovery came out with deep emotion.

"I am here to tell you that one person on the outside is seeking to forgive the man who crushed the life out of her cherished daughter, and, in the name of Christ, wants him to feel loved and prized as a human being."

Her words, her tears, her transparency were shattering. In the silence that followed her address, a man stood, identified himself by name, and said, "I am the man you are waiting to forgive." She gasped, totally taken aback by this surprise. Tears filled her eyes . . . and slowly she opened her arms. The man at last came to the platform. They embraced. Her journey of offering forgiveness was nearing its end. His journey of finding it was just begun.[2]

## Notes

1. Dorothy Sayers, "The Devil to Pay," in *Masterpieces of Religious Verse* (New York: Harper, 1948), 189.
2. Adapted from David Collins, *The Vintage Voice* (newsletter, Church Pension Fund), 1991:1.

## 3

# HOW IS FORGIVENESS POSSIBLE?

August 25, 1993, the day before she was to leave Capetown, South Africa, to fly home to Newport Beach, California, Fulbright scholar Amy Biehl was beaten and stabbed to death. The killer, nineteen-year-old Mongeszi Manquina, had just come from a rally at his high school held by the militant wing of the Pan Africanist Congress, a black nationalist party opposing Nelson Mandela's African National Congress.

"One settler, one bullet," speakers exhorted hundreds of students. The young man, with a group of about eighty, were marching together, chanting, waving political banners, and singing when they spotted the yellow Mazda 323 with a white girl at the wheel. A brick crashed through the windscreen. Amy jumped from the car and tried to run for cover from the hail of stones. Manquina caught up and tripped her. Her black friends and coworkers ran from the car shouting, "She's a comrade, she's a comrade." But the killer had already borrowed a pocket knife.

The killers—arrested, tried, and convicted in 1994—were pardoned four years later by the Truth and Reconciliation Commission. The parents, Linda and Peter Biehl, were present for the amnesty hearings. They supported the young man's bid for freedom. "We understand," they said. Their daughter Amy would have forgiven him, they believe, and they have too. In the courtroom, Linda looked across to see the young man's mother, Evelyn Manquina. She was wearing an Amy Biehl Foundation T-shirt (the foundation Amy's parents created to work at antiviolence through education, community development, and recreational projects that support social change and the teaching of nonviolent values).

Linda caught the other mother's eye across the room. They pressed through the crowd and hugged. "The message that was sent out [by that hug] sent electric shocks down your spine," says retired Archbishop Desmond Tutu.

"To be honest, I don't have it in me to hate the killers; I just don't," Peter, the father, says, and Linda interjects, "To me, I never personalized it with the killers. I think you can say who really is responsible for this killing. You go back to the creators of Apartheid." But for the Biehls, they find that their response of forgiving cannot really be explained. The first trip to South Africa they went to visit the mother of Amy's killer in her concrete block house. After the meeting, they emerged to see a rainbow across the sky, like the promise of the ancient Basotho proverb they had just heard quoted: "Out of ruins, good will come." What happened in that moment is inexplicable, but "it was like grace fluttered into our hearts."

## Not Something We Do; Something We Discover

Pastoral counselor John Patton once explained this concept to me in a quick synopsis of his excellent book, *Is Human Forgiveness Possible?*[1] by saying (as I wrote down his words later that night), "Forgiveness is not something we do; it is something we discover. I am able to forgive when I discover that I am in no position to forgive. I am more like those that hurt me than unlike them, more similar than different. Forgiveness is not the act of canceling a debt or erasing an act of wrongdoing; it is the discovery of our similarity. It is all right to be like someone else, even the one who has done us wrong."

He quoted Elijah the prophet's humbling discovery of his own humanity and fallibility: "I am not better than my fathers" (1 Kings 19:4 KJV).

Forgiving is something we discover, something "like grace fluttering into our hearts" as our viewpoint slowly changes. It is a viewpoint because it requires the changing of the mental view and the emotional point of departure (where we start from) in remembering the injury.

Changing the viewpoint involves reframing the memory. The picture of what was done is still clear, but the frame is new. We set it in a new context, the context of a new understanding of the other and of a new understanding of how similar we ourselves are to the one who has hurt us. The person who was offended does not violate the facts of the injury in doing this—the picture is still the same in its ugliness or evil—but the frame sets the injury in a new place, permits seeing it in a new context, and allows us to view it in a different light.

This discovery of a new frame does not come easily. It is not a sudden acquisition of magic eyes or the quick removal of cataracts. Rather, it is like an inexplicable recovery from shock, loss, or grief. Gradually one finds that new understandings open the heart to further capacity to be more understanding.

It is not a pseudoanalysis that creates a psychological explanation—a rationalization—for the other's actions that exonerates or excuses. That is an intolerable game played by those who mimic Job's comforters in seeking to fix the pain through reductionistic solutions offered with the best of intentions but the worst of consequences.

Instead, it is a growing recognition that one does not need to fully understand another to be understanding of his inner pain. Perfect understanding of another is no guarantee of compassion. "To know all is to forgive all" is true only where there is unconditional love, and in the final accounting, only God can love unconditionally. Our best efforts only allow us to reduce the conditions to the minimum possible, but they do not achieve the absolute none of *un*. We cannot, we do not, we will not know all or understand all in order to forgive all. But we can be understanding, offer understanding, risk extending understanding even to those who have hurt us deeply.

The new frame of an understanding heart may awaken compassion even for the offender. This does not include any condoning of the evil done, but it refuses to preclude the worth of the person or to exclude him from the human community as an "animal." One can view another through the frame of understanding no matter how violated one has been or how violating the hurtful memory may be when recalling the doer and the deed. Rage and outrage still well up as one recalls the injury. In unexpected moments, unanticipated signals trigger painful memories that return one to the pain event. But compassion wells up too. This is not an end to be reached once and for all, but a process to be entered, joined, and rejoined.

## The Search for an Understanding Heart

"I'll never forget the look of white anger, shame, and terror that filled Lori's eyes that night," her mother told me. "She came through the door disheveled, distraught, and I knew what had happened— what I had feared. Date rape. She had begun seeing this guy, who seemed a good person to her and to us. But old friends who'd never interfered before would drop a word of warning. No one gave details, just vague caution. We tried to dissuade Lori, but our opposition only drove them closer. Then one night their intimacies accelerated. Lori tried to stop it, but he grew violent, forced her, dropped her off a block from home, and fled town—leaving her guilt-ridden, depressed, violated, and pregnant.

"Finally, through his mother, we discovered that he was with his estranged father in another city. They brought him back. He acted repentant enough and asked to see her alone to talk things out. Instead, he became violent again, this time beating her severely before he was restrained.

"Lori was hospitalized with a severe concussion and shock. For days in deep depression, she wanted to die.

"The boy? Two weeks' detention, a few interviews with a social worker, and he was free. Now today I learn that he's got an acquaintance's daughter pregnant, and they're getting married.

"I lie awake at night burning with anger and bitterness. True, Lori's recovering. The baby's adopted into a good home. Lori's entering college in another state to get away from it all. But the scars go deep to her soul. The old buoyancy and trust are gone out of her. And when I see it, I feel everything in my own soul turning to hate.

"I can't express the feelings I have toward this—this thing who ruined our lives. Isn't there some way I can heal the hurt of all this?"

❧   ❧   ❧

There are injuries so deep that no understanding is sufficient to engender compassion. Although we know that even when someone has done a terrible wrong there is more to him than that single misdeed, it is only head knowledge. The decision to search for any seed of compassion left on the floor of our soul takes courage, courage to not give the other a double victory—once in the injury and second in our souls. Beyond the discovery that we can refuse to turn the other person into a monster lies a second discovery. We can see the other as blind, yet still invited into the light; as a doer of evil, but as more than the evil that he has done.

Even our best intention "to understand," to decipher the other person's formula, to unravel the mysterious tangle of emotions and motivations can become an exercise in hypocritical superiority. We are tempted to indulge ourselves in impugning the other's motives, prejudging his attitudes and actions, and stereotyping him as fitting into the set of cubbyholes we've constructed—classifying and permafreezing him into a neat category. Playing God.

In being understanding, we accept the complexity of human motivation, the contradictions in persons that are beyond our explanation. We realize that there are ambivalences and inner tensions we will not be able to explain but can visualize as part of the human condition, complex and terrifying as it often is. This capacity to understand what is beyond understanding is something we value in others, and it's what others often value in us. Paul wrote that having love—being understanding—is greater than possessing great insight. "Even though you understand all mysteries and all knowledge but have not love, you are nothing" (1 Corinthians 13:2, paraphrased from the KJV).

Any offender, whatever the offense, deserves the basic human effort on any other's part to offer a modicum of understanding. We can go beyond reacting to what others do or how they act and begin to respond to what they are, to what they want to be, or to what they could become if only in our exploratory thoughts. The heart will say no long after the will has begun to say yes to such thoughts. In time, all three—head, heart, and will—will approach each other and together walk the painful road toward forgiveness.

Radical disagreement can exist alongside deep understanding of another. One can refuse the one and increase the other. Blind to this paradox, a young man criticized his dad, saying, "He doesn't understand me, or else he'd see things the same way I do." It may be that the dad disagrees because he understands all too well. Rather than *agreeing* with, it's seeing with the other, *seeing* things from the other's point of view whether you believe it is valid or not. It may also be *feeling with, responding to* the other's emotional reactions, whether they seem reasonable to you or not. Understanding is not unconditional acceptance, but it is acceptance in foreign conditions.

## Valuing the Other

When one looks again at an "unforgivable" man and recalls that he *is* a man, one possibility is to ascribe value to the person. This is possible particularly when one realizes that ascribing value is only a preliminary step to the deeper recognition. Human beings do not have ascribed value; they have appraised value. Their value lies not in the eye of the beholder, but in their created worth. God does not prize us in spite of our worthlessness, but appraises us as worthful. Worth is not *bestowed* by grace, it is *affirmed* by grace. Our value is rooted in creation, not in redemption. The highest unit of value in the universe is a human soul (Mark 8:36–37).

No one is totally without worth, even the enemy. My enemy is also a person for whom Christ died. No one for whom Christ died can be to me an enemy, an object of hate or scorn. God valued each person more highly than He valued His own life. If I love God, how can I keep from loving my sister or brother (1 John 4:20)? The other is a person for whom Christ died, meant to be a child of God, with the possibility of becoming a saint as well as a demon. No one (however irresponsible) is too low to be an object of God's love. No one (however evil) is excluded from the forgiveness of God, except as one excludes himself by unrepentance. No one can be considered worthless when Christ—God Himself—died for him. No one is ultimately unlovable. If God loves her, then God can love her through another person who embodies God to her.

## Loving the Other

The third step toward forgiveness is loving others. Before the real work of forgiveness can begin, understanding and valuing must be expressed in restoring perceptions of love. To love is to see the other as precious regardless of the wrong done or the injury felt.

Ralf Luther writes: "To love one's enemy does not mean to love the mire in which the pearl lies, but to love the pearl that lies in the mire. By seeing the other with new eyes, by restoring perceptions of worth, by recognizing the other's preciousness in spite of a particular behavior, you can glimpse the pearl glinting through the mire."[2]

"How can you keep on loving and forgiving your brother?" I asked a man who stubbornly continued to break through in his alcoholic sibling's losing battle with addiction.

"I think the turning point for me was the night I went to pick him up at a local dive, and he exploded in violence," he explained. "It was when I faced his glassy-eyed stare. He lifted his hand to strike me, and hatred, anger, and revulsion flared up within me.

"Then I remembered—was it a kind word spoken when we were boys and trying to survive our alcoholic dad? Or was it the tender affection he showed to me the day my own son was born? I don't know, but right there I knew that the man I used to know and love was the real man, not this one before me.

"Now I cannot look at him without seeing the empty, desperate captivity that holds him. My forgiveness and love may be his only link to God. How could I withhold it?"

To give love to another is both a negation and an affirmation. As a negation, we face the unhealthy, destructive, ill-motivated, unacceptable behavior head-on. We do not condone the offense or overlook the wrong done, but we refuse to consider this behavior as a measure of what the person is in his or her deepest self. As an affirmation, we assert that this person has worth no matter what choices, actions, or mixed intentions are visible. We affirm the healthy, the constructive, the right motivated, the responsible center of the person. We choose to affirm and to believe that this is the real, the possible, the capable, and the accountable core of the person. We claim and reclaim the real center, no matter what has surfaced in our relationship.

Where there is love, what was done is separated from who has done it. In working through our mutual repentance, mutual change of attitudes, and mutual reconstruction of the relationship, this negation and this affirmation go hand in hand, step by step. We step forward on one assertive foot, gain balance, then place forward the affirmation. Often this happens in small but increasing increments, step by step, until the journey of restoring love, recognizing repentance, reclaiming relationship, and reopening the future has been completed.

Understanding, valuing, and loving are all steps toward forgiveness. They are not yet forgiving, but the prerequisite steps toward forgiveness. The real work of forgiving begins when an attitude of love has been restored. Then the negotiations of trust can begin resolving anger, suspicion, and resentment, and reopening the future. This is the difficult task that gets bypassed when forgiveness is made cheap, private, and one-way. Real forgiveness is more costly, more demanding, deeper. Real forgiveness comes with the recovery of a relationship, even when the rupture is repeated again and again.

In describing such understanding, such valuing, such loving, the negation is as crucial as the affirmation. Love is the balanced tension between union with the other in affection and separation from the other in respect for the safety and security of both self and the other. It is moving as close to the other as is possible without violating the other's worth, dignity, or personhood. It is moving as close as possible without violating the self. It is the balance between negation of all that is destructive and invitation to reconstruction. In the case of the deep physical, emotional, and psychological trauma of abuse, the abused may not and often should not return to relationship with the abuser. In the case of rape, the victim may not, and in most cases, should not reestablish a relationship with the rapist. However, as is true in other cases of destructive aggressive behavior, for the sake of the spiritual, emotional, and psychological healing and growth of the abused one, there is a need to work through several steps of the forgiveness process.

She or he may find that dialogue with the perpetrator, in a context of safety and with the presence of persons who safeguard emotional, spiritual, and physical security, can bring about levels of healing that can be reached in no other way.

If a woman is in a marriage or a family where there is physical or psychological abuse, counsel that in the name of spirituality recommends forgiveness, denies the violence being done, and overlooks the exploitation being endured, is actually spiritual abuse.

She deserves recognition of the evil being done to her, intervention in a relationship that is toxic, and the opportunity to reclaim her life in a healthy space. In most cases, she should seriously consider removing herself from the danger or the abusive person.

She needs the safety of separation, and the separation may cause the abusive person to realize that his violence is tearing the home apart.

Understanding the other, valuing the other, and loving the other does not mean being in subjection to, enabling the abuse of, or complying with the destruction of the self, the child, or the family unit. Instead, it can be the basis of moving toward the needed intervention, the reality of caring enough to confront so that the possibility of mutual caring can be envisioned, pursued, and perhaps, someday realized. If this stage is not a possibility, then fully grieve for the loss that represents and the tragedy it is.

### Notes

1. John Patton, *Is Forgiveness Possible? A Pastoral Care Perspective* (Nashville: Abingdon, 1985).
2. Ralf Luther, as cited in Helmut Thielicke, *Life Can Begin Again* (Philadelphia: Fortress, 1963), 75.

## 4

# CAN FORGIVING
# BE LEARNED?

It was in a church in Munich that I saw him—a balding, heavyset man in a gray overcoat, a brown felt hat clutched between his hands. People were filing out of the basement room where I had just spoken, moving along the rows of wooden chairs to the door at the rear. It was 1947 and I had come from Holland to defeated Germany with the message that God forgives.

It was the truth they needed most to hear in that bitter, bombed-out land, and I gave them my favorite mental picture. Maybe because the sea is never far from a Hollander's mind, I like to think that's where forgiven sins where thrown. "When we confess our sins," I said, "God casts them into the deepest ocean, gone forever. And even though I cannot find a Scripture for it, I believe God then places a sign out there that says, NO FISHING ALLOWED."

The solemn faces stared back at me, not quite daring to believe. There were never questions after a talk in Germany in 1947. People stood up in silence, in silence collected their wraps, in silence left the room.

And that's when I saw him, working his way forward against the others. One moment I saw the overcoat and the brown hat; the next, a blue uniform and a visored cap with its skull and crossbones. It came back with a rush: the huge room with its harsh overhead lights; the pathetic pile of dresses and shoes in the center of the floor; the shame of walking naked past this man. I could see my sister's frail form ahead of me, ribs sharp beneath the parchment skin. *Betsie, how thin you were!*

The place was Ravensbruck and the man who was making his way forward had been a guard—one of the most cruel guards.

Now he was in front of me, hand thrust out: "A fine message, Fraulein! How good it is to know that, as you say, all our sins are at the bottom of the sea!"

And I, who had spoken so glibly of forgiveness, fumbled in my pocketbook rather than take that hand. He would not remember me, of course—how could he remember one prisoner among those thousands of women?

But I remembered him and the leather crop swinging from his belt. I was face-to-face with one of my captors and my blood seemed to freeze.

"You mentioned Ravensbruck in your talk," he was saying. "I was a guard in there." No, he did not remember me.

"But since that time," he went on, "I have become a Christian. I know that God has forgiven me for the cruel things I did there, but I would like to hear it from your lips as well. Fraulein,"—again the hand came out—"will you forgive me?"

And I stood there—I whose sins had again and again to be forgiven—and could not forgive. Betsie had died in that place—could he erase her slow terrible death simply for the asking?

It could not have been many seconds that he stood there—hand held out—but to me it seemed hours as I wrestled with the most difficult thing I had ever had to do.

For I had to do it—I knew that. The message that God forgives has a prior condition: that we forgive those who have injured us. "If you do not forgive men their trespasses," Jesus says, "neither will your Father in heaven forgive your trespasses."

I knew it not only as a commandment of God, but as a daily experience. Since the end of the war I had had a home in Holland for victims of Nazi brutality. Those who were able to forgive their former enemies were able also to return to the outside world and rebuild their lives, no matter what the physical scars. Those who nursed their bitterness remained invalids. It was as simple and as horrible as that.

And still I stood there with the coldness clutching my heart. But forgiveness is not an emotion—I knew that too. Forgiveness is an act of the will, and the will can function regardless of the temperature of the heart. "Jesus, help me!" I prayed silently. "I can lift my hand. I can do that much. You supply the feeling."

And so woodenly, mechanically, I thrust my hand into the one stretched out to me. As I did, an incredible thing took place. The current started in my shoulder, raced down my arm, sprang into our joined hands. And then this healing warmth seemed to flood my whole being, bringing tears to my eyes.

"I forgive you, brother!" I cried. "With my whole heart."

For a long moment we grasped each other's hands, the former guard and the former prisoner. I had never known God's love so intensely as I did then. But even so, I realized it was not my love. I had tried, and I did not have the power. It was the power of the Holy Spirit recorded in Romans 5:5, "...because the love of God is shed abroad in our hearts by the Holy Ghost which is given unto us" (KJV).[1]

➤    ➤    ➤

This marvelous story from one of the great apostles of forgiveness and reconciliation is particularly intriguing since it is, on careful reflection, not about forgiveness; it is about love. The gift that she receives at that moment of soul-searching confrontation with the old guard is the gift of love that enables her to perceive him once more as a fellow human, as a precious person in spite of his terrible wrongdoing, as one who is loved by Christ and therefore within the realm of possibility for her acceptance. As she reports, the miracle of that moment was the return of love to her hand, her arm, her heart.

But a second thing that the story holds out in bold relief is the necessity of learning to love, of relearning to love, of unlearning our unlove, and of learning again to love what has seemed unlovable. When the other is seen as beyond all boundaries of inclusion, outside the circle of those who can be loved, one must return to the humbling awareness that while we were yet enemies, in some way beyond our explanation, we were loved of God. And it is in this love of God that we find the model, the motivation, the slow budding capacity to restore love for the other in small, yet growing, measure.

No matter how often we have forgiven or have been forgiven by others, we are still learning to forgive. Forgiveness is not a skill that is mastered and becomes second nature. It must be faced each time injury or injustice strikes.

Forgiveness is not a gift one claims, internalizes, and then possesses for life. It must be rediscovered in each situation of pain. We never grow beyond the learning stage; we never go beyond the level of student.

No one is a master here. We are learning to love unconditionally; we are discovering how to work out the conditions of forgiveness.

In Corrie ten Boom's open confession of anger and love, of resentment and release, the first steps of forgiveness are visible in the compressed tension of a surprising confrontation. The first steps are all she has the opportunity to explore. Before she could take the third and fourth steps there would need to be conversation. She would need to say, "I remember you. I was there. I was injured. My sister died there. You were part of that. We must talk." Then repentance would become a possibility. Forgiveness is the mutual recognition that repentance is genuine and that right relationships have been either restored or achieved. It is not denial of the injury, avoidance of the conversation, pretence that it does not matter, generosity that overlooks the reality of actual wrongdoing, tolerance that permissively sidesteps the hard work to be done, superiority that rises above the other in magnanimous perfectionism. It is the hard, painful, vulnerable risking of sharing in the conversation on repentance.

Forgiveness is not an act—it is a process. It is not a single transaction—it is a series of steps. Beware of any view of instant, complete, once-for-all forgiveness. Instant solutions tend to be the ways of escape, avoidance, or denial, not of forgiveness. Forgiveness takes time—time to be aware of one's feelings, alert to one's pain and anger, open to understand the other's perspective, willing to resolve the pain and reopen the future.

The steps of forgiveness are:

1. *Restoring the attitude of love.* To love another is to see that person as full of worth and precious regardless of any wrongdoing. This is not forgiveness, although most writers and pastors call it such. It is the prerequisite step. Forgiving cannot begin until love has been re-extended to the offender. Love is possible when we see the other's

value once more, recognize his preciousness, and choose to be understanding, even of what is beyond being understood.

2. *Releasing the painful past.* To accept another is to meet him or her now, as the person she really is. To hold the past between us as if it could be undone or to demand that what was done must be redone is fantasy, not reality. To come to terms with reality is to accept the past as past. Obviously, what has happened has happened, but emotionally it is still taking place. In anger we struggle with the illusion that we can turn time backwards and run it all through again, that we can make the other undo what he or she did. I am not my past; I am a person capable of repenting, changing, and turning away from past patterns of behavior. You are not your past; you are equally free to change if you accept the freedom that is within you. To affirm that freedom is the first step of forgiveness.

3. *Reconstructing the relationship.* This is the real work of forgiveness. To review the pain of offense within each of us and between the both of us is not easy, but it is the way to healing. As we work through our anger and pain in reciprocal trusting and risking, at last we come to recognize the genuineness of each other's intentions. Our repentance needs to be authentic, honest, and as complete as possible at the moment. That is the central work of forgiveness. "If your brother wrongs you, reprove him; and if he repents, forgive him. Even if he wrongs you seven times in a day and comes back to you seven times saying, 'I am sorry,' you are to forgive him," says Jesus in His most succinct and clear description of essential forgiveness (Luke 17:3–4 NEB).

4. *Reopening the future.* This is the consequence of transforming the memory from a wound that will not heal to a wound that has healing power within the soul. The relationship may return to a civil participation in community with mutual respect, or to a new level of friendship resulting from the depth of encounter that has taken place; or it may mean a return to or the beginning of profound trust and willingness to risk. In each case, the future is reopened to whatever level of relating is appropriate to the two participants. Not every relationship should be pursued. Not every forgiveness leads to a continuing conversation between the two. Not every healed injury will result in the resumption of the previous relationship. There is a time to say "Good-bye" and a time to say "Hello" and a time to say "May the Lord watch between us as we part from each other in mutual

respect and friendly parting." But the future is open to possibilities we do not yet see.

Forgiveness, by definition, is the mutual recognition that repentance is genuine and that right relationships have either been restored or are now achieved. The ratio of repentance between two estranged persons is hard to define. But the two can find their way until both recognize that the overtures are genuine in intention. Perfection in performance is not a suitable criterion, Jesus insists. Even when a person fails repeatedly to hold true to his intentions and returns with recurrent requests—seven times in one day—we are to accept on the basis of sincere regret.

Charles William, the English theologian, has written on this: "Who decides? Whether repentance is indeed repentance? Or whether it is fear or greed or hate masquerading as repentance? Must we? In fact we do because we must. No doubt in the end only God knows all, and we may forgive a hypocrite or reject a penitent. The danger of the last is the greater."[2]

The demand for an ironclad guarantee that will fix all future acts permanently and securely and insure our safety from any future pain must be canceled. No one can offer such assurance and go on living as a truly human being. Such promises of perfection are possible only for saints or statues, and neither is desirable in a relationship. In the future we will be spontaneous together. We may fail. We may act hurtfully again.

5. *Reaffirming the relationship.* Reconciliation must end in celebration, or the process has not ended. We must touch each other as deeply as is possible in our release of the pain and then celebrate the mutual recognition that right relationship has now been restored or achieved. This bonding of renewed acceptance and mutual affirmation allows us to meet with a new meaning to our relationship. To end a reconciliation negatively—"May God help us that this never happens again"—blocks our growth as persons. It is fascinating that the words of mistrust and suspicion Jacob and Laban set between them—"May the Lord watch between you and me, when we are parted from each other's sight" (Genesis 31:49 NEB)—have been transformed in following generations into a benediction of love and a celebration of relationship.

## Forgiving, Forgetting, Forgoing

Returning to Corrie ten Boom's marvelous story, after exploring the steps of forgiving, we may ask, "Did she forgive the prison guard?" No. She took the steps possible at that moment, but she herself describes it as steps one and two. Love was extended; the past was recognized as past. Before real forgiveness could take place, the two would need to remember the pain together, recall the injury together, recognize real repentance together, and agree to forget together.

Theologian Frank Stagg writes insightfully about authentic forgiveness:

> Forgiving and forgetting are related, but forgiving precedes forgetting. To forgive, one must first remember the injury, the impact, the injustice done.
>
> To forget ignores the needs of the offender and injures the offended by driving the sense of being wronged deep into one's own being where resentment does its slow destructive work. Forgetting is negative, passive; forgiving is positive and creative.
>
> Before one can forgive and forget, both offender and offended must remember together, recall the wrongdoing together, finish the feelings together, reconstruct the relationship together and then they may forget together. In the remembering, reconstructing, forgiving and forgetting each regains the other.[3]

To insist that forgetting come first is to make passing the final exam the entrance requirement for the course! How often have you been told to "forget and forgive" and then kicked yourself because you couldn't? The more you tried to forget, the better your memory!

Just as with insomnia, the more you attempt to stop the mad race of thoughts, the swifter they fly. The person who struggles blindly to forget only sears the thought more deeply into the memory.

Forgetting is the *result* of complete forgiveness; it is never the *means*. It is one possible consequence, and not always a desirable one.

To say, "I can forgive, but I can't forget," may sometimes be saying, "I know how to overlook a wrong but not to forgive it." But more often it is the frank recognition that memory cannot be silenced by any act of the will, and though the memory remains to teach us, the meaning of the event undergoes change.

Now, let's be clear—forgetful forgiveness, when it does occur, is not a case of holy amnesia that erases the past. Instead, it is the experience of healing that draws the poison from the wound. You may recall the hurt, but you will not relive it. No constant reviewing, no rehashing of the old hurt, no going back to sit on the old gravestones where past grievances lie buried.

True, the hornet of memory may fly again, but forgiveness has drawn its sting. The curse is gone. The memory is powerless to arouse or anger. It was said of Lincoln, "His heart had no room for the memory of a wrong." Forgetting sometimes follows forgiving. But it is not essential, not the most common conclusion to reconciliation, not a skill to be learned, not a final state to be recommended or demanded.

The past is the past. Nothing can alter the facts. What has happened has happened forever. But the meaning can be changed, the consequences can be altered, the future can be reopened, and the rapport can be restored.

To "for-give" is, in the English language, an extended, expanded, strengthened form of the verb *to give*. By intensifying the verb we speak of giving at its deepest level, of profound giving, of giving from the center of the soul, of *giving forth* and *giving up* deeply held parts of the self.

To "for-give" is a process of *giving up*. In forgiving we give up demands for perfect behavior, perfect justice, perfect resolution, perfect retribution. All we can ask of ourselves and the other is genuine repentance. In forgiving we give up the angry picture of the wrongdoer. We put aside the view of the other as an unworthy, unacceptable, unforgivable offender. In forgiving we lay aside the view of ourselves as righteous and the other as totally unrighteous, and we begin to experience the truth that we are both fallible humans in need of being forgiven.

To "for-give" is a process of *giving forth*. In forgiving we give a new trust to another, exemplified by our risking being open, vulnerable, and available again. We allow the future to come meet us without constricting its flow through ironclad guarantees of perfection or fearfully frozen limitations on our spontaneity. In forgiving we give forth a new freedom by believing in the other, by accepting fully the genuine worth and intrinsic value of this person who is as much a child of God as we are.

In giving up, we *forgo* revenge and *forfeit* recriminations; we *for-*

*bid* old resentments and *forbear* strategies of getting satisfaction for the injury. In giving forth we *foresee* an open future in our relationship; what we cannot *foreknow* we can still *foretell* out of our commitment to *forgive*. In *forgiving* we *forsake* old patterns of brooding review and move toward *forgetting* the pain and remembering the healing. In *forgiving* and *forgetting* we *forge* a new relationship.

By using the series of intensified words that begin with *for*, although there are many more, we are recognizing the depth of effort, feeling, and commitment required in the work of forgiveness.

## Forgiveness Is Rare, Hard, Costly

Forgiveness is far more rare than one assumes at first thought. More often it is not forgiveness that occurs, but pious denial, memory fatigue, polite avoidance, or deliberate subterfuge.

I recall a painful moment when I replied to a request for healing too quickly with the words: "Will I forgive you? Why, of course! I've already forgiven you. Forget it; it didn't matter!" The man had come to me with a serious apology. And what did I say to him? "It didn't bother me. I didn't take offense about what happened back there."

What did I mean by that? Was I trying to tell him his actions and insults couldn't hurt me? I mean, who did he think he was? Of course I forgave him. And I felt quite good about it until my conscience put on a demonstration, shouting, *Unfair, hypocrite.*

*Whadda ya mean?* I protested. *I forgave the guy, didn't I?*

*Uh-uh,* my conscience said. *You just said you did. You only winked at it. You didn't really forgive him. Not yet.*

*Now wait a minute. When have I refused to forgive anybody?*

*Oh, you haven't refused; you just avoided it. This time you pretended it didn't matter, but that's not what I overheard you tell your wife. And did you forgive that woman last week? You're still brooding over a measly little criticism. And last month—*

Forgiveness is rare. It is rare because it is difficult. It is difficult because it is costly. The cost may require us to risk further hurt by exploring the injured relationship with someone who caused the injury to begin with. The cost may be that we will have to absorb pain without any satisfactory release and restoration. The cost may require us to accept further rejection when the other brushes us off, blames us further, burns us with additional anger, or blatantly refuses to talk.

So often there is no way to open the conversation of reconciliation. Western society has become so exaggeratedly individualistic that forgiveness has become superficial. It is tolerance or indifference to others. In such a failure of relationship it is tempting to call our forgiving attitude "forgiveness" and go on. Yet the relationship still lies broken.

If we take Jesus' concern for forgiveness as going to the brother or regaining the sister, then we will not reduce forgiveness to an attitude instead of an action. Where the actions of reconciliation are not possible, we feel the failure of the relationship, but we do not excuse it by calling it forgiveness. Often the most we can do is to invite the other to conversation.

Among the learnings that follow from this, here are several I consider central, which are expressed in "I Language."

- *I* must respect the other's right to refuse to converse. Perhaps he feels overpowered. The power differential between persons can make resolution difficult or even very problematic. Perhaps there are reasons from long past that make this resolution more painful than this person can bear at this time.
- *I* will honor her "No" and feel the failure, whatever her reason may be. I will feel the failure of the relationship and remain open for real forgiveness to happen sometime in the future.
- *I* will recognize that the new relationship will be different from the previous one. Often it may be richer because we have now met at a deeper level than before. Or we may renegotiate the relationship to a less intimate level that is more appropriate to our needs. When a marriage is ruptured, forgiveness may mean the restoration of the marriage; or it may mean the renegotiation of mutual respect at the level of friendship or shared parenting as single parents. But the anger can be resolved, the pain faced and released, and the relationship resumed at an accountable level.
- *I* must learn to forgive, relearn to forgive in the next instance, and be willing to unlearn past ways of forgiveness that are no longer effective or satisfying.
- *I* will learn to forgive, not for my good mental health, my rest at night, my dignity before a critical conscience, or my private release, but for the restoration of relationship and the renewal of community.

⋟  ⋟  ⋟

Once a group of students asked their teacher, "Rabbi, how can we know when the night has ended and the new day has begun?"

"What have you been taught?" he asked.

"It is the moment when one can tell the difference between a sheep and a goat," one said. "No, it is the moment when one can differentiate between a white thread and a black one," reported a second.

"Neither are right," the rabbi replied. "It is the moment when you look in the face of someone you have known as your enemy, and you can see that it is your brother or sister. Until that moment, no matter how high the sun has risen, it is still night in your soul if you cannot see who is truly standing before you."

### Notes

1. Corrie ten Boom, *Tramp for the Lord* (Old Tappan, N.J.: Fleming H. Revell, a division of Baker Book House, 1974), 55–57. "I'm Still Learning to Forgive" by Corrie ten Boom. Reprinted with permission from Guideposts Magazine. Copyright © 1972 by Guideposts, Carmel, NY 10512.
2. Charles Williams, *The Forgiveness of Sins* (London: Faber & Faber, 1950), 198.
3. Frank Stagg, *Polarities of Man's Existence in Biblical Perspective* (Philadelphia: Westminster, 1973), 161.

# WHAT ABOUT THE INJURY, HURT, AND ANGER?

Three coffins—the mother's, the fathers, and the daughter's—stand together at the front of the church. Three of the four surviving children sit in the front row. The fourth is in prison, charged with the three deaths.

The congregation of mourners witnesses a surprising ritual. An aunt reads a message from the children present to their absent brother.

"Alex, you are our brother. You will always be our brother. We are all in great pain. This time of suffering is no time for us to be angry with each other. We know that you share our remorse at our parents' tragic death. We will be with you in love during the difficult years ahead of us all, but especially those stretching out before you. The pain we all bear is too great to understand, but we love you; we forgive you."

Having read the statement, she joins the family in bringing little bunches of violets as symbols of forgiveness to lay inside the coffins.

Tomorrow morning, in his Oregon prison cell, the brother—who will speak only to his court-appointed attorney—will pick up the paper to read the account of their actions of acceptance. His stony silence and withdrawal will open a crack, they hope, in the fifteen-year-old's wall of rage.

❧   ❧   ❧

Jonesboro, Arkansas. The Sunday morning after the tragic shooting of school children by school children in this middle-America city—a tragedy of gigantic proportions that has an entire nation in shock and grief—the people attending church hear a puzzling set of sermons. In most of the churches that morning the messages, as reported by attending reporters, address the same theme.

The messages are not on the question of why a loving God permits such evil in the world, nor on the enduring mystery of monotheism—how the one and only all-powerful, all-knowing, just, and loving God allows such horrendous evil to occur, even amid the little children.

Nor are they about the dilemma of our arming ourselves as a people to protect ourselves violently against anticipated violence—and in the process becoming like those we fear, accepting the same tactics, using the same weapons, feeling the same rage, and bequeathing it to our children who carry it out in life.

Nor are they about the transformation of our just anger into action for justice. They do not address the rightness of feeling deep anger at the circumstances, the context, the culture of violence, and our own complicity with the worship of violence and death that nurtures the atmosphere that produces the young marksmen and feeds the myths that direct their shots.

No; the sermons demand that Christians forgive the children's murders and murderers. The ministers do not simply deliver the message that though we cannot explain such suffering, God is with us as we accept the pain and are grateful for what we once had. Grateful while our hearts cry out in lament and anger for children now lost, a heroic teacher who sacrificed his life to protect them, the heritage of priceless memories, and the hope that God will call them to life in the resurrection. No, instead the preachers feel called to preach the demand that at this moment, in spite of our loss, pain, anger, sadness—and much, much more—we must forgive the murderers of our children. Does this not seem brutal? Or out of touch with the heart? Or disconnected from reality?

What can this teach us about our understanding of forgiveness?

About our denial of loss; about our pain, suffering, and failure—about evil itself? What does it say about our flight from our anger and about the recognition of justice and of just anger? Does it show us anything about our own denial of our true feelings?[1]

❧    ❧    ❧

"Sometimes I wonder if I can ever forgive him," the wife says as we sit around the kitchen table. "I know it's too early to think of that. I'm still getting in touch with how much anger I have. That will take me quite a while."

The forgotten teakettle whistles a forlorn note from the old wood range. The man in question sits, eyes downcast, speechless before her anger. We sit in silence. I can see by the set of her jaw that she is reliving one of the many scenes of outrage, like the day last week when she and her daughter drove into town to confront "the other woman," as the pulp magazines always put it.

They rang the doorbell and waited. Then the woman stood framed in the screen door, squinting at the daylight, slowly recognizing her callers. Her knuckles glinted white on the doorknob. Her face was an impassive mask. All parties stood mute in mutual hate.

Then the daughter broke the silence. "I've wanted to see your face for years," she said, "and now that I've seen it," she continued, and spit on the ground, "you make me sick." Then mother and daughter turned powerlessly away, aware that they should not have come, that they had nothing to say but the futile words of anger, anger that belonged more to the father/husband than to his partner.

I'm remembering this scene years later. In the years that passed, the other woman married and moved out of his world. Slowly, bitterly he paid, repaid, and overpaid for all he'd done, for all of his wife's anger. At last, one night when she herself was deep in trouble, lonely and desperate, she offered her forgiveness. And his moment for giving back the futile anger had finally come.

"You can keep your phony forgiving," he told her. "I don't need any of it now. I've paid through the nose for what I did. Who needs forgiveness when he's already paid?" Then he poured out his disgust that had been the original motivation for the angry affair, had festered all through the years of his and his wife's cold war, and now emerged in false triumph to step on her again when she was down.

✒    ✒    ✒

Destructive anger drives people apart, severs relationships, settles into the floor of the soul, contaminates all other feelings and through them thoughts, choices, and acts. Destructive anger freezes the normal processes of grieving into pathological mourning and ices over the depths of the soul.

Constructive anger seeks to break through the walls, yearns to remove the barriers, presses to open communication, mobilizes energy to work at injustices, and searches for opportunities to reach out to the other in genuine contact.

Both types of anger exist within us at all times. We have a choice—and not just between anger and denial as we are taught in childhood ("shame on you for being angry; don't feel it; don't feel!"). This is a real choice between destructive anger and constructive anger; between negative rage and the positive outrage that seeks to change a bad relationship, an irritating situation, a malignant way of communicating, an evil bind.

Central to the work of forgiveness is the task of working through our feelings of destructive anger. In the stories just told, there are many forms of anger. In the first story, there is the anger of the bereaved children and the sorrow of a family driven underground by the community's need to "forgive and forget" by seeking an immediate resolution of a situation that will take years of healing for all involved.

In the Jonesboro story, much must be done to make things right. Families have lost their children, parents have lost their trust in those who became child-killers, a school has lost its innocence, a town has lost its purity, and a nation has lost its faith in institutions. These wounds must all be addressed and the anger faced and turned from negative, fruitless blaming to positive, creative change for all possible.

In the third story, anger that is bitterness and rage must be resolved. The anger of the man who betrayed his wife, the rage of the wife he betrayed, the hostility of their disillusioned daughter, the alienation experienced by "the other woman," the malice of years spent spiting one another, the bitterness of exacting repayment, and the wrath of long revenge in cold coexistence—all these show how anger takes many forms in human tragedies.

## Varieties of Anger

There is a rich variety of anger emotions. To describe them "in color" is to see a whole spectrum. Red anger is an immediate flash of healthy temper; purple anger is congested, inhibited, and internalized; blue anger is becoming depressive and despairing; black wrath has turned toward destructive goals; and white rage sees nothing but its own cold, calculating desire for the annihilation of the other. Few of us allow ourselves to feel more than red anger without quickly denying what we feel and avoiding what we really long to say or do.

Or anger may be described as a range of temperatures.

At the bottom of the thermometer is the icy, cold, irrational hostility of frozen hate. Going up, the cool antagonism of continued animosity and long-held grudges appears.

Then, at more normal temperatures, are common, ordinary touchiness and irritability. You recognize the symptoms—raw sensitivity, impatience at the least difficulty, instant sharp words.

From here, the mercury soars. There are hot flashes of temper that flare out like bursts of steam. These can turn to boiling, scalding anger —the blood rises, the neck and face redden, and the ego will not allow anyone butting in. And the thermometer pops its top when anger explodes into physical violence, which is the high point of anger, as we lash out in assault, abuse, and even murder.

With such a spread from the frigidity of hate to the fever of rage, the emotion of anger should be one of our best understood, most carefully managed, and most effectively channeled emotions. It is much too powerful to be overlooked, much too dangerous to be ignored.

Yet it is one of our least-understood emotions and most misunderstood motivations. Since we understand it so poorly, we direct it easily in negative spirals, destructive directions, and malignant pathways instead of harnessing its potential for constructive transformation.

Both poles of anger are aroused within us as we feel demands in binding situations. Anger is the energy mobilized by demands. Whenever one views the environment as full of demands, "feeling energy" is experienced as anger. Demands turned outward create anger. Demands turned inward create guilt or shame.

"Anger demands" may arise from many contrasting situations. They can arise out of jealousy, when a guy you don't like lands the big job you wanted. Or they can be prompted by outrage when another steals a promotion from someone who deserved it by floating rumors that spoiled the other's chances. (The first is a vain demand; the other a just demand.)

Or "anger demands" may spring from the resentment we feel when we goof and the other guys rub it in. (Nine out of ten cases of anger are sparked when someone pricks our self-conceit.)

Or they can spring from the outrage we feel when someone insults, criticizes, or pokes fun at a friend's business ability, intelligence, manners, or taste.

They can be the result of the blind anger we feel when a job goes wrong, when things break down, when work piles up. Or they may express the frustration we feel when we just can't handle a situation or feel inadequate to perform some needed task.

In each of these situations, the anger springs from some frustration and emerges as just or unjust demands that can be pursued to seek new justice or canceled to return to a balanced acceptance of reality. These demands may be cries for justice and thus deserve expression. Or they may be pretentious, godlike requests for unlimited attention, deference, dominance, protection, privilege, or entitlement and should be recognized as inappropriate and exaggerated demands that deserve to be canceled.

There are just, morally authentic, truly unselfish reasons for anger—anger when another is misused or abused, or anger over an injustice done to you. This is valid anger with just demands, and it deserves careful reflection and purposeful expression and negotiation. Then there is a self-absorbed, self-centered anger that is concerned only with the self and its narcissistic demands.

Anger as an emotion can be good or bad, helpful or harmful. Which it is, is totally dependent upon the reasons for the anger and how it is exercised.

Anger as an out-of-control explosion is most often an unnecessary evil, hurtful to you and others. Such anger may be a violent desire to punish others, to inflict suffering, or to exact revenge. But anger in itself—a normal, truly human emotion—is a morally neutral source of human energy, arousal, and excitement.

If anger can be right or wrong, how can you judge it when you possess it or you discover it seems to be possessing you? Have you been taught to simply reject all anger out of hand, lumping it under the uncomplimentary title of "sin"? In your family of origin was anger a vice, or was it sometimes a virtue? In far too many families in many cultures, anger is too quickly treated as shameful. Most people are early taught to lie rather than admit they are angry, as though anger were the king of evils, the vice-chairman. ("I am not mad," they say. "Of course I'm not angry.") Or they'll deny it in midsentence, like the man I overheard yelling, "I AM NOT RAISing my voice!"

## Creative Anger

Anger can be harmful to us—physically, medically, emotionally, and socially. But it may be transformative, regenerative, and renewing—in reforming a person, in driving her to shake off slaveries, in inspiring him to risk new possibilities, in empowering her to attempt new goals and make something of her life.

Anger can be harmful to others in striking out at their personalities, hurting their self-esteem, or damaging their emotional balance. But anger can be a great service to others, too. It can challenge injustice or right wrongs that oppress others. It can blaze out with a pure force against evil. The latter is the potent anger of an Abraham Lincoln who, seeing the slave market at New Orleans for the first time, reportedly said, "Let's get out of here, boys. If I ever get any chance to hit this thing, I'll hit it hard."

Consider the blazing anger of a Tolstoy against class oppression, violence, and war; of a Gandhi against the domination of his people, the exploitation of his land, and systemic and political oppression; of a Martin Luther King against racism and social and economic injustice.

Disciplined anger is dynamic, potent. There is a moral center, a central place in the soul, for such anger. When we no longer feel deeply, care passionately, or speak forthrightly—even heatedly—about justice and what is right, when "anything goes," when everything is tolerated, all is lost.

Disciplined anger focuses its demands on what is just and on what is good. It rises above the ordinary irritations of life to seek secondary change in relationships, systems, covenants and agreements for living, the rules and organization of marriages and parenting, and the way communities include value and free minorities and genders. It is disciplined because it discards the primary demands for personal safety and security that normally dominate our thinking in order to press for those values that endure beyond the moment, that outlast our life-times, and that reach beyond ourselves.

Mohandas Gandhi, the great Indian leader and teacher of non-violence, had this motto on his wall at Sevagram:

> When you are in the right,
> You can afford to keep your temper;
> When you are in the wrong,
> You cannot afford to lose it.

Seneca, the ancient Greek philosopher, wrote, "He is a fool who cannot get angry, but he is a wise man who will not!"

If you use anger rightly, it will give your life stamina, with its motivation to work for justice and its determination to act with principle and conviction. But if you allow anger to use and abuse you, it can warp and twist your life and mental health. *Use* anger. Do not let it use you. Live out your depths of thought and feeling. Do not let them live your life for you. Learn to live reflectively as a responder, not reflexively as a reactor.

One of the strange and tragic things that happens to the multitude of so-called ordinary people as they move through the developmental journey of life is that they become complacent, compliant, and confluent. They forget how to be indignant. Obviously, this is not because they are overflowing with human kindness, but because they adjust to life, accustom themselves to what must be, settle for what is. When they see evil and injustice, they are pained but not revolted. They mumble; they rarely cry out. They sin by omission by not becoming angry.

Yet their anger is the one thing above all others that could make their lives truly count. Few of us have the resources or the moment in leadership to launch crusades or initiate reforms, but we can contribute to the conditions in which crusades can be effectual and reforms successful. The wrath of the multitude can foster civility, decency, and integrity in public life. It can freeze the atmosphere in a way that will silence the prejudiced demagogue or the jaundiced rumormonger.

## Purposeful Anger

Effective anger, focused anger, clarified anger, clearly articulated anger, distinctly moral anger, creative and reconstructive anger is our hope, our power for change, our incentive to grow, and our courage to act.

One of the most poignantly human, genuinely centered stories of clarified anger is the account of an event that occurred in the early ministry of the young Jesus, when he exploded in open, justified anger. Encountering a man with physical or conversion paralysis, feeling empathy for his pain and need, surrounded by legalistic, uncaring spectators who stood poised like vultures to criticize His compassionate and free service to others, He showed vivid anger at their rigid, unfeeling bondage to unjust traditions. He looked at them in unequivocal anger, expressed His demands pointedly and provocatively, and acted decisively.

> Then he said to them,
> "Is it right to do good on the Sabbath day, or to do harm? Is it right to save life or to kill?"
> There was a dead silence. Then Jesus, deeply hurt as he sensed their inhumanity, looked round in anger at the faces surrounding him, and said to the man,
> "Stretch out your hand!"
> And he stretched it out, and the hand was restored as sound as the other one. (Mark 3:4–5)

His anger was principled, not personal; it was about values and virtues, not about persons and personalities. It was not about the particular wrongdoers, but about the wrong done to others and the abuse of the weak and helpless. These abuses ignited His indignation; this was anger in love. Anger and love are compatible. In fact, love without anger is as worthless as anger without love. The opposite of love is not anger; it is indifference. The opposite of anger is not love; it is tolerance.

## Channeling Anger

Anger is not prohibited in the Bible. It is affirmed when it is channeled, critiqued when it is undisciplined, and modeled in stories of both varieties. The apostle Paul's words (which open with a quotation from David's command in Psalm 4:4, which Paul cites and then contradicts) are the best summary of the wisdom of scripture on handling such live emotions.

If you are angry, be sure that it is not out of wounded pride or bad temper. Never go to bed angry—don't give the devil that sort of foothold. ...Let there be no more resentment, no more anger or temper, no more violent self-assertiveness, no more slander and no more malicious remarks. Be kind to one another; be understanding. Be as ready to forgive others as God for Christ's sake has forgiven you. (Ephesians 4:26–27, 31–32)

Commentary on these concise highly condensed words of emotional wisdom:

*Be angry—but beware.* You are never more vulnerable to evil than when you are angry. In anger, self-control is stretched to its ultimate capacities. Common sense works better at low temperatures. Reason decreases as your emotions rise.

*Be angry—but be aware.* Anger soon soars to illusions of power, sinks to resentment, turns bitter. It can lead to temper, hatred, and malice.

*Be angry—but be caring,* the text concludes. The anger that is motivated by love of neighbor, love of the right, and love of God is worthy; it is worth the risk. Its demands are focused on justice, restoring relationship, and opening communication, so learn the virtue of caution. When you are angry, examine your demands carefully. Don't give them the benefit of the doubt.

The Bible recommends intensive self-exploration and points to the inner conflicts that invariably precede interpersonal confrontations.

But what about the feuds and struggles that exist among you—where do you suppose they come from? Can't you see that they arise from conflicting passions within yourselves? You crave for something and don't get it; you are murderously jealous of what others have got and which you can't possess yourselves; you struggle and fight with one another. (James 4:1–2)

In anger, one gets a rare chance to see the shadow side of the hidden self momentarily exposed, sometimes revealed sharply, unretouched. Look and learn. Your anger may be an index to inner conflicts unattended to, unfaced, unresolved. Or your anger may be an unconscious admission of guilt-demands still unaddressed in the personality—false guilt from conventional demands that can be faced and dismissed, or moral guilt that can be owned, confessed, and released.

Anger is a common sign of those inner conflicts that boil up from bad consciences, oppressive super-egos, inner-tyrant representatives of abusive parents or authority figures that maintain levels of self-punitive rage or repressed guilt. A racist is more outraged by a charge of prejudice than the person who knows his or her biases. A thief is far angrier at being accused of theft than is an honest man. It's more often the adulterer than the faithful spouse who flies into a rage when an affair is revealed. Anger can be far more revealing than even your conscience's inner warning signals.

When you feel anger mounting, ask yourself, *What is my demand? How am I demanding change? What do I really want?* An honest answer is like a dash of cold water to the temper, a cup of cold water to the soul.

On the other hand, check out the anger that pleases you. It may be the jealousy, envy, or hatred in you that preens itself in fulfillment whenever the person who triggers these emotions suffers a touch of humiliation. It may be inordinate pride that delights in the satisfaction of watching another putting down the person who once made you lose face. It may be that nothing feels quite as good to you as the righteous anger you feel when the other deserves a subtle nudge to justice. When you begin to enjoy warming up to anger, ask yourself, *Why?* If you can't find the answer, if your inner feelings of hostility are inexplicable, or if you find yourself constantly irritated, negative in outlook, critical, and hostile, then, by all means, sort it out with someone else—someone who knows the language of the soul—a counselor or pastor.

Leon Saul, psychiatrist and author, wrote: "I believe [that] man's hostility to man is the central problem in human affairs . . . that it is a disease to be cured and prevented like cancer, tuberculosis, or small-pox, and that its cure will result in healthier, better living—not only for society in general but for each individual in particular."[2]

Hostility is an illness when it is always just under the surface, easily aroused, and constantly making a person irritable, touchy, critical, scapegoating, or angry with an impotent rage that's fueled by everything and flares up over nothing. Anger is an illness when it is used to accomplish childish goals or to bulldoze through normal conflicts where cooperation, compromise, and understanding should be enough to solve the problem.

Chronic inner hostility is a disease—a disease that results from unwholesome pressures that warp a person's thinking and emotions. Inner anxieties, blocks, frustrations, and guilt feelings can cause hostility to smolder unconsciously in your soul. When it comes to anger, we're not all created equal. Tempers vary widely. It may be that one person will control as much temper in a given hour as another in a lifetime. If we remember that good spirits are much easier for some than others, we will be a bit less critical.

What a difference in temperaments among Christ's closest friends! Take the contrast of Peter and John, for instance. It may have taken as much grace to keep the apostle Peter from knocking someone down on the street as it took to make John look like an angel of love!

### Releasing Anger

Release from anger comes from *owning* and *opening*. Own your feelings. They are your responses to your perception of your situation. Own them as your "response-ability" at that moment in that situation, with all of the anxiety, pressure, energy, and exhaustion you brought to the event. Own your responses to those also involved in the interaction, or to those whom you may have hurt by your hostility. And recognize that all owning before ourselves is at the deepest level owning before God. God, who already knows our innermost, is our eternal and gracious Witness.

To summarize these reflections on owning, channeling, and utilizing anger constructively, a few guidelines may be worth further reflection:

1. *To channel anger, slow down.* Learn to delay your responses. Set a later time to settle a conflict or misunderstanding. This is one of the few good uses of the habit of postponing. Put it off till later. Then emotions will cool off, the head will clear, and good judgment will return.

2. *Don't put it off too long.* Set strict limits on the delay. Don't do a long, slow burn over anything. Getting mad may be necessary sometimes, but remaining mad never is! So don't store up an unfinished anger agenda. Keep close tabs on yourself, and balance all your books by the end of the day. "Let not the sun go down upon your wrath," the Bible wisely exhorts (Ephesians 4:26 KJV). The poison of hostility is bad enough in your conscious mind; don't force it down into your subconscious by sleeping on it. Keep up-to-date accounts.

3. *Learn to be honestly open with anger problems.* Go to the person with whom you were angry. Straighten it out. Life is too short to be ruined by bitter grudges and continuing indignation. Learn to go and make things right—humbly and graciously! One of the best ways of controlling anger is to talk the problem out with a friend or even yourself. Talking to the mirror, keeping a journal, facing yourself in your own favorite way is indispensable. Dr. William Menninger counsels: "Do not talk when angry. But after you have calmed down, do talk. Sometimes we push each other away and the problem between us festers and festers. Just as in surgery, free and adequate drainage is essential if healing is to take place."[3]

4. *Examine each anger situation.* Ask yourself, *Exactly why did this touch off my temper?* Self-understanding is a key to anger prevention. Do your best to be understanding of the other person, too. And be sure you understand the true situation between you. It's seldom what it seems to be. All these steps may help you defuse the explosives in your personality.

The help of an understanding counselor may help you understand how and why these feelings have risen. A minister can guide you in accepting God's forgiveness. Then you can accept yourself and go on to full forgiveness of others. Through growth in your spiritual journey, you can discover that there are resources of love suitable to your own spiritual style of faith for transforming anger in the discovery of depth in forgiving and being forgiven.

Making peace with your own anger and being at peace with another's right to be angry are two qualities that free us to be effective reconcilers. Since forgiveness is, at its heart, the resolution of anger within and between people, it is the person whose anger is accepted, channeled, and directed appropriately who can take the first steps toward peacemaking.

➤   ➤   ➤

Martin Luther King Sr., the man affectionately called "Daddy King," was the father, not only of his famous son, but of the civil rights movement in America. As one leader said at his funeral, "If we started our own country, he would be our George Washington."

In his eighty-four years, Daddy King endured a great flood of hatred. To mention only a very few of these hate events: During his childhood in Georgia, he was an eyewitness to lynchings of other African-American men. The first time he tried to register to vote in Atlanta, he found that the registrar's office was on the second floor of city hall, the elevator was marked "whites only," the elevator for "blacks" was out of order, and the stairwell was closed. But the great hate tragedies of his life were two murders. His son, the leader of the civil rights movement, was cut down by James Earl Ray's assassin's bullet. Then, six years later, Marcus Chenault stood up in the congregation and began shooting as Mother King was playing "The Lord's Prayer" at the organ. She fell dead in the hail of gunfire while Daddy King watched in horror from the pulpit.

Near the end of his life, Daddy King was asked whether he hated the people who had killed his wife and son. He replied, "Nothing that a man does takes him lower than when he allows himself to fall so low as to hate anyone. There is no time for that. To hate is to live in the past, to dwell on deeds already done. Hatred is the least satisfying emotion, for it gives the person you hate a double victory— once in the past, once in the present. As long as you hate, you are chained to the past."[4]

### Notes

1. Adapted from Jacob Neusner, "It's Too Soon to Ask Forgiveness," *Los Angeles Times,* 31 March 1998. Jonesboro, Arkansas, quotation.
2. Leon J. Saul, *The Hostile Mind* (New York: Random, 1956), 14.
3. William Menninger, "Behind Many Flaws of Society," *National Observer,* 31 August 1964, 18.
4. Adapted from Martin Luther King Sr., with Clayton Riley, *Daddy King: An Autobiography* (New York: Morrow, 1980).

*6*

# WHAT ABOUT APOLOGY AND CONFESSION?

I can't tell her; it would end our relationship," the man said to me, fingering the moisture from his eyebrow. "Under no conditions will I tell my wife. She'd never forgive me, and, well, that's just the way it is. She can't even overlook a little thing like, well, just coming home late. Any slipup and she'll bring up the date and time of day for every other time I did it."

"But you asked for this conversation to explore how you *would* tell, not *if* you would tell, right?" I asked.

"Yes, so I said, but I can't face that now. I can't tell her. She'd lose her temper, slap me once, and walk out—no, I can't. I know what I want to do, but that is not the same as what I believe I can do."

He was on his feet and backing toward the door.

"You know what you want to do. Perhaps that is enough for one conversation. Can we talk again?"

"Yes, oh, yes," he said, and he was gone, carrying with him the story of marriage and marriage conflicts, of two careers, two schedules, two independent businesses developed into two mutually exclusive lives, pursuing two widely separating trajectories.

They had lived the happy marriage–happy family dance in front

of their friends and larger family while his work grew more important and success exploded in the wife's business. Regional adminis-
tration fell into her lap. Money began flowing more freely. Two-day
absences grew into four-day conventions.

Fortunately for her, a friend with time to care for the kids was
available as a nanny for the kids, then as a chef for the husband, and
gradually a friend to the lonely as proximity, mutual conversations,
and the chemistry of evenings under the same roof turned friendly
chats into intimacy, and camaraderie became infidelity.

Then the youngest child caught rheumatic fever. The schedules
and values changed, and the tensions between the couple began to
snarl and knot beneath the surface. With both women sometimes
around the house, he fled it in fear, plunged himself more deeply
into his work, but nothing silenced the nagging whisper of guilt,
the fear that she would find him out and that the scandal would ruin
their family, reputation, home, and life.

The next day he was back, and I knew from his face that he had
told her, and yet somehow his fears had not come true. "It was after
dinner," he said, "when she asked me point-blank, 'What is it about
you tonight? You're like you haven't been for years.' What was I to
say? I was, well, speechless. And before I knew what I was doing, I
had told her. Told her what I'd done to her and to the kids. Told her
it was with her friend.

"She sat, head in hands, until it was all out. Then she asked, 'Is it
really true?' 'Yes,' I said. 'And is that all?' 'Yes.' The silence dragged. My
heart had stopped.

"Then she stood, stepped behind me, and touched my hair. I
looked up to see tears. 'Let's start over from here,' she said. 'Can we
start a new life, somehow, something different, start over together?'

"It was too much for me to take. I looked away; my hands were
like iron on the arms of the chair. Then—then I began to shake; my
teeth ground together for a moment before I caught them; everything
blurred.

"'Why,' she said, seeing me trembling and white, 'why, you're angry.' I nodded my admission. 'You wanted me to hit you, didn't you?'
Slowly I nodded that she was right.

"'No,' she said, 'if I hit you, that would make you the bad boy
and me the evil mother and it would only justify everything you
did. And probably have touched off both our tempers for the last

time. No, no; we've got to work at it, work it out; it's our only hope if we're ever going to live again.'

"That's when healing happened," the man told me. "Her accepting me like that, it, well, it broke my heart, or it broke down my last resistance, my last self-justification. You see, I was still blaming her and her work and busy schedule for my unfaithfulness. And her forgiveness was so unexpected; it was like she was someone I hardly knew. She gave me back my life."

Could he have found forgiveness without confession? Certainly he had to confess it to someone. To a friend who would be understanding and help him face his problem in honesty; to a pastor who represented his community of faith and could guide him in working through the multiple relationships he had violated; to God, the only true source of forgiveness and release.

But to his wife? Not all marriages are alike; not all persons are equally capable of handling such blows. One should be cautious in prescribing general rules for all situations. One should view with suspicion those rules that lump all interpersonal situations into a single category. But in the betrayal of a marriage, the partner has a right to know what affects at least five key dynamics—the partner, the self, the marriage relationship, the children, and the other person. The adultery was committed against the spouse, against the couple's marriage, against the two of them as a unit. And in particular, it affected them *both*—and both will be necessary to making it right.

The first hopeful sign for this marriage was the husband's recognition of wrongdoing and his ending of secrecy and denial—what is best called *repentance*. If he repents, that is, honestly and completely turns away from his wrong actions and ends the unfaithful relationship, how far must he go in confession? Certainly confession will bring a tremendous release and relief for his tortured feelings of guilt. But it then places the weight of the pain on the shoulders of the spouse. What will she do with this painful information and insult? Will she be able to forgive, forget, and accept him again? Will the confession be constructive, bringing healing and health once more to their relationship? Or will it be a block that nothing will be able to remove for her? Will it embed hostilities in her soul that she is not emotionally, spiritually, and mentally able to overcome? Will it be constructive or destructive of love, understanding, and acceptance?

In family counseling, years of working with such injuries to trust, loyalty, faith, and integrity, all point toward encouraging not more deception as a proposed cure, but an end to deception. In the healing of family injury, our faith must be in an open system, not a closed system. Individual solutions grow out of individualism as a perspective on self, spirituality, and the relationship between persons who are atoms of separate distinct choice. We may once have believed in individual solutions in our worst exaggeration of our culture's worship of the individual as a sole center of responsibility—the adolescent myth that often fuels teenage search for identity. But more sober adulthood recognizes the web of relationships that create true personhood.

So what do we say pastorally about the need for, the extent of, and the uses of confession? Classically, pastors and pastoral counselors proceed from the following common assumptions.

*Confession should be as public as the commission of the act.* Those directly involved have a right to know—a need to know—and should be included in the confession. Sin should not be published for general public consumption and speculation, but it will have to be clearly addressed with those involved in trust relationships if trust is to be restored.

*Confession should be shared where it is a help to another, not an unnecessary hurt or a moral, relational, or emotional hindrance.* If confessing your sin creates the occasion for further wrongdoing—providing another with desired justification for oft-threatened abuse or carrying out warnings of retaliation, or is an attempt to further hurt the other by defiantly flaunting the insult implicit in the wrongdoing, then it needs further counsel and self-examination.

*Confession should not be so intimate, revealing, or painful that it will wound or scar the person to whom it is confessed.* Such careless, thoughtless confession to a close friend or lover may bring you release, but it will transfer the painful burden to the other. One person is healed at the expense of another. It is rarely wise to confess by "telling all," down to the small details, to your most intimate friends. Go first to a Christian friend who cares but would not be personally harmed. Any brother or sister who knows how to live openly in the light can hear your confession and help you in finding the next step in repentance and reconstruction of the relationship.

If you should choose not to confess to those involved in your life and explain the choice as being for the sake of the limitations of the other in being the acceptant or for the sake of being redemptive and loving to the other person, be aware that you are choosing the harder, not the easier, way. To make such a judgment about the other deprives him or her of the truth. Truth deprivation is crazymaking and ultimately destructive of the personality and the relationship. To live with the unspoken memory of your sin, to find some sort of unilateral forgiveness without sharing the meaning of that forgiveness, is not an easier way. It is all the more demanding of you and your own spiritual and emotional journey.

This is true because, essentially, confession is a human necessity. Truth is as necessary to us as air. Integrity is the nourishment of all healthy relationships. All true spiritual growth comes from the acceptance of fallibility, not the pretense of perfection; from the acceptance of diversity, not the illusion of our sameness in denial of personal choices; from the facing of consequences and the owning of our failures, not the pseudosafety of concealment. We discover and experience release from our guilt (a necessary and indispensable word that names a very real and valuable feeling and state) in direct proportion to our willingness to face our sin, confess our sinfulness, and accept forgiveness.

## Confession Accepts Guilt as a Gift

Guilt is a much-maligned emotion. It is one of our most painful feelings, most hated experiences, and earliest sources of intense discomfort. The internalization of inner controls cannot be achieved without the activation of this primary human capacity. However important it may be in our socialization and our learning of moral values, it is experienced by normal persons as an unwelcome punishment from an inner parent who cannot be silenced or easily satisfied. Yet guilt is not only necessary for healthful living, it is a gift to be used wisely as well, not simply a burden to be lifted.

For most persons, the normal and healthy capacity to feel guilt is something to be prized, and the content of our guilt deserves to be explored, expressed, and released. However, for many, an unwelcome guilt accumulation within may stretch back to our third and fourth years when the first guilt feelings began to emerge from our early childhood sense of shame and were not released constructively but stored semipermanently. Guilt is the gift that lasts a lifetime, we sometime remind ourselves ironically.

Guilt reserves may slowly and persistently deposit an emotional residue from the frustration caused by parents who shouted, "No, no, no"; by brothers and sisters who chanted, "Naughty, naughty, naughty"; and by teachers who demanded, "Now aren't you ashamed of yourself? You shouldn't have done that." Much of this collected guilt is constructed from false fears that should be forgotten. But within this storehouse of guilt feelings there is the capacity for authentic guilt, which is a necessary process of inner direction.

Guilt, we come to recognize as we enter adulthood, can be true guilt, which when faced can be forgotten as it is forgiven. It can also be false guilt, which may be faced but is not easily forgotten because its causes are not easily available to rational reflection.

The roots of such feelings can lie in fears of rejection by an internal jury composed of a large cast, or they can be grounded in internal structures of self-punishment that accept no resistance and yield to no protest. Such feelings are best worked through with a counselor-guide who knows the territory of the soul.

When guilt is a sense of wrongdoing, an emotional conflict that arises out of second thoughts on something we have done, then it can be, not *un*done, but *re*done through recognition and repentance. If we have violated our accepted moral or social standards, or even if we imagine we have violated them, the accusing voice within us that cries "Guilty!" can be addressed and silenced.

Guilt, with all its complexities, is a nagging voice that is insistently nattering on in the background until we attend to it carefully and seek to discern its real demands for change. Trying to identify these may be somewhat like wrestling an octopus in a darkened aquarium at midnight.

## Confession Explores All Four Floors of Guilt

Guilt may be usefully pictured as existing on multiple levels within the personality. We may, as a metaphor, describe it as a museum with galleries on four floors.

The main floor of this three-storied guilt is the area of normal experience and interchange with people. Here, in the court of social opinion, we become aware of our guilt before others. This is *conventional guilt* that comes from violating or failing to keep the social rituals or conventions of family or society.

Since our first feelings of guilt do come from others—stimulated in a child's mind when parents scold—they spring from the fear of the loss of a parent's love. As the circle of significant others widens, so does the number of guilt-inducing authorities. All through our maturing years, our fear of the taboos of our family and friends gives birth to guilt feelings. These vary, of course, according to the moral and social standards that are found in our society.

An African bush mother might feel guilty if she does not throw a set of identical twins to the jackals. Yet, in other communities, such a mother would be guilty of murder. But in all societies, when a member falls short of the requirements of life with others, he or she loses face on the outside and feels guilty inside. This guilt before others, or *social guilt,* arises whenever a person's actions are blameworthy in the social environment. Such guilt may be true or false, depending on the taboo involved.

The second floor of guilt is the guilt of unrealistic feelings—what is more often called *neurotic guilt.* It is guilt before an internal judge and jury in the court of the mind (or often the imagination). The critical self can be a most lenient judge, or it can be mercilessly cruel. Some individuals are capable of mastering the art of conducting their inner trials cleanly and with dispatch, leading to decisive actions to correct their failures or mend endangered relationships and thus lead a healthy emotional life. Their feelings of guilt are dealt with promptly, clearly, and forthrightly.

But other persons find that the judge claims ultimate authority, pronounces exorbitant sentences, and requires them to depress themselves by elaborating on their blameworthiness. They feel forced by the inner tribunal to build vast storerooms of guilt feelings reaching many stories into the sky.

The third floor is the arena of *true moral guilt*—actual guilt for things done wrongfully or things undone in negligence. This is not just a guilt we face in the court of our minds or in the court of public opinion. This is guilt that requires an answer before the moral values we have learned, the ethical norms of our community, and the deeper texts of moral authority, such as the Holy Scriptures, which provide the basis for historical, universal moral reflection and orientation.

This is the floor where we meet true guilt, the place where we become the responsible self, the place of authentic moral agency and action. Here we find the arena for weighing the significant decisions of our lives, our relationships, and our ultimate commitments. This is also the holy place for conversation of the conscience with God. Here we take our actions with ultimate seriousness, with eternal perspective on guilt as we recognize that moral guilt is not just before self and others, but also before God.

We—all of us—are "sinners" (certainly no one can argue long about that). We have all sinned and fall short of the goodness intended for us in the Creator's design for wholeness (see Romans 3:23). We are at one and the same time free to sin and bound to sin! We are not sinners because we sin; we sin because we are sinners.

For many persons, the fourth floor is unknown and unexplored. It is the floor of what we call—for want of a better name—*existential guilt*. This is the deeper stuff of the soul. This is guilt that is a sin against what you might do, might be, might become if you took your *life* with the kind of seriousness it deserves, your *possibilities* with the depth you could have invested, your own *soul* with the profound reverence it deserved.

Here one asks the questions, *Why have I failed to be all I could have been? What of the roads not taken, the opportunities not seized, the life that passed unlived?* This is not an imaginary attic of guilt; it is the heart of our failures. You and I are truly guilty here, deep down in our personalities. Down where we failed to spend time reflecting on our personal destinies and refused to direct our lives away from pursuing immediate or intermediate goals to search for the ultimately important.

On all four floors, there are feelings of guilt that are legitimate and illegitimate. Each of us needs to spend time and effort to sort out which is true guilt and which is false guilt. One needs some trustworthy point of reference for making such judgments. Culture, society, fashion, popular opinion, and pseudoscientific norms serve for many. Research findings and polls of normality become the last word. But the deep unease of such a base for one's life awakens a hunger for a deeper bedrock. One can return to the rock beneath all other rocks, the Holy Scriptures, and seek to be accountable before them on all four levels of moral and social behavior.

"The Bible illuminates our problem in a remarkable way," said Swiss physician Paul Tournier in his book *Guilt and Grace*. "From now on, 'false guilt' is that which comes as a result of the judgments and suggestions of men. 'True guilt' is that which results from divine judgment."[1]

## Confession Claims the
## Healing Power of Community

Community surrounds us, shapes our lives, and guides our formation of values, but it often is not available when we need it most—in our times of failure. Yet community is not just the ever-present *context* for our healing; it offers the basic *content* of that healing process.

It is there at the most basic level of our understanding of how healing comes, what it requires, and where it begins. It shapes our most basic understandings—even our understanding of the Bible. No one reads the Bible alone. An invisible community of commentators and interpreters sits with us each time we open it. Each of us understands and interprets its teaching from a particular moment in the centuries and from a particular culture and context; we seek to build a bridge of understanding between the biblical world of two thousand years ago to our present situation.

We cannot do that alone—we *do* not do it alone—since two thousand years of earnest interpretation and application shape our understanding, whether we are aware of it or not. We each need a circle of cotravelers to test our understandings and commitments. This is called the church. When the church is being the church, it supports persons in discerning the truth for their lives, incorporating it in their practice and experience, and finding what is truly, as Tournier called it, "divine judgment."

As you direct your life honestly within open dialogue with fellow believers in Christian community, you will discover a safe place to deal openly with the problems of true guilt in your life. You will also find support in claiming the freedom that liberates yourself from the false guilts suggested and assigned to you by people and the pressures of friends and foes. There you can find a context to move away from isolation with your failures and toward repentance and forgiveness.

Authentic guilt should move us toward regret through remorse to the re-creative step of repentance. When this happens alone, as it often does, we may be able to move into the freedom we seek. But such freedom most often comes when we can discuss and declare our intention to change in an important relationship with others. All lasting change, let us note again, is a change within relationship. That is where it takes place, finds its validation, gains its firm resolve, and is incorporated into the life of the person.

A caring community can help one move from being sorry about failure to taking creative action; and that step, obvious as it seems, is not as easy as it may appear. The leap from sorrow to action can be a high jump with an unreachable bar. Paul the apostle praised his Christian friends at Corinth because their sorrow led to repentance and release. Listen to his words: "The result was to make you sorry as God would have had you sorry. . . . The sorrow which God uses means a change of heart and leads to salvation—it is the world's sorrow that is such a deadly thing" (2 Corinthians 7:9–10).

## Confession Transforms
## Sorrow to Constructive Change

Sorrow sours quickly into the bitter misery of blind regret. *Oh, if it never had happened!* But what can we do? Roll back the clock? Undo the deed? Impossible! Remorse repeats its routine of regrets and reprisals. If a guilty person never gets beyond this point, sorrow does more harm than good. It turns into anger at being caught, fear of being found out, or frustration that others "got away with it."

"The sorrow which God uses means a change of heart." That's repentance. A change of mind and heart. It is necessary for release of guilt; more, it is the basis of right relations with God.

In repentance, the heart is not only broken *for* its sins but *from* its sins. Mere sorrow, which sits and weeps out its regret, is not repentance. Repentance is sorrow converted into action. Right actions in the future are the only true apologies for wrong actions in the past. To claim repentance without revolution of life is like continually bailing a swamping boat but never plugging the leak.

"To do so no more is the truest repentance," wrote Martin Luther. True repentance is a change of direction. It is not only a mental matter, but an action as decisive as spinning on your heel and turning toward a complete change in purposes and pursuits. Remorse will cause a person to halt repeatedly but then continue in the same path. Repentance is an about-face. It is a turning from sin and a turning to God in believing faith.

## Face the Soul

To face your own soul is to discover openness. This honesty that comes from simply taking inventory of your life with another person as witness allows one to see the truth without self-punishment or self-justification and find the courage to do something about the unfinished and unresolved contents within. The courage to face the soul and do something about failure, stupidity, and sin leads to the next step.

The soul is the inner voice, the depths of the "heart," the inwardness that knows your own preciousness, suffers when devalued or injured by others, and grieves its violation by your own blunders and blindness. The soul is the center that remains when one strips away all posturing and pretense and stands as the person you truly are before God, and you do this best when it happens in the presence of another person who knows God and loves you as a fellow child of God.

## Clear Out the Soul-Clutter

The accumulated debris—the junk of the memory, mind, and heart—can be dealt with and discarded. Historically this is called—plainly and simply—*confession*. To confess your undesirable and embarrassing collection of old issues that bind you is to risk the threat called honesty. Spiritual freedom and emotional release come through finding the appropriate path for such admissions. This may include confession of regret to the one wronged, or sorrow and the clear intention to change expressed to the Christian friend who is standing by you with love and concern, or a more public statement to a group of people—if they are the ones you have involved in your sin.

Recognizing the path that is necessary to get to the place you want to be seems an obvious step, but it is the missing element in so many conversations on clearing the clutter of old business. Process is as important as content in resolving inner as well as interpersonal conflicts. We are wise when we are tough on process and soft on people, are clear on how we will work at claiming freedom and righting old wrongs, and clear on giving care to all concerned.

## Walk Away

Leave the past behind. You are not your past. You are who you are now becoming.

Let go. Show that you possess the willingness to say good-bye to the old identity and are eager to embrace the new. When you have named the problem, cut off the old attachment to it that connected it to your identity. I am the one who failed, not the act of failing. I am the fail-or, not the failure. I am the doer who did the deed I regret, not the deed. I am the actor, not the action. I have disowned that way of being, have disconnected from that style of behaving, have turned in a new direction, and have claimed a new identity by cutting old identifications to past loyalties. I am committing myself to a new center.

### Walk a New Walk; Dance a Different Dance

Live the freedom; live out forgiveness! True freedom through confession has two sides. Confession with only a negative side is emotional nudism. It's the admit-your-failures-and-get-them-off-your-chest variety of pulp fiction or popular press. But true confession has a positive side, a new way of walking, a new dance of joy. It is a confession of hope in new relationships, delight in new freedom, and trust in the new ability to live in honest openness.

Once you have faced the worst about yourself and discovered grace and release—once you have admitted your helplessness, weakness, and need—you then are free to claim this positive side. Exploring the negative is necessary if one is to move into the positive. Do you recall how David describes this change in one of his songs?

> When I kept silent,
>     my bones wasted away
>     through my groaning all day long.
> For day and night
>     your hand was heavy upon me;
>     my strength was sapped as in the heat of summer. Selah.
>
> Then I acknowledged my sin to you
>     and did not cover up my iniquity.
> I said, "I will confess my transgressions to the Lord"—
>     and you forgave
>     the guilt of my sin.
>                                     —Psalm 32:3–5 NIV

The new walk opens the door for future conversations about our human fallibility (since it will be with us all our lives) and about future mistakes (since they will recur if we go on living). Such conversations are a part of the new walk, the joyful dance of open forgiven and forgiving living. And they too happen not in secrecy but in relationships and in the community of the spirit which honors confessing people.

"When the Bible talks of confession," writes William Klassen, "it never describes a simple mental process, but always an activity that takes place in public. We confess with our lips!"[2] It further says "Confess your sins to each other and pray for each other" (James 5:16 NIV).

When I stand before my sister or brother honestly, as I truly am; when through authentic confession I bring my humanity, my struggles, my failures out into the light; something dies—my false self and its endless self-justification is broken. My defenses fall. My guilt is uncovered, the light reveals it, and it dies.

In contrast, my refusal to confess—that is, to live honestly and openly in the light—is actually walking in darkness, living a lie. To pretend perfection and peace where in reality there is hidden guilt and secret sin is not human. True humanness owns and celebrates humanity by seeking the full humanity seen only once, in one Human Being, in the One named Jesus. He is the mirror of true humanity and the perfect window to divinity.

✴   ✴   ✴

During World War I, an American prophet and social reformer, Eugene Debs, was imprisoned as a conscientious objector. He was placed in a cell with the most feared prisoner—an African-American man who was considered incorrigible, devoid of any spark of goodness, totally isolated from others in his rage. He had spoken to no one since his imprisonment, responded to other inmates with only cold disdain and visible hatred—especially for whites, who had been the source of lifelong discrimination and oppression.

Debs quietly observed this rage for a period, then began a totally nonverbal process of stealing past the man's defenses. He began to drop half the things brought to him by visitors onto the man's cot when he wasn't looking, to act out the equality he believed, to show respect in the most subtle but unmistakable and undeniable ways.

Gradually the rebuffs decreased, the first words of communication were uttered, the rejection ended, and the two began to tell their stories. Friendship had begun.

Years later, now a minister and community leader on the outside, the man received word of Debs's death.

"He was the only Jesus Christ I ever knew," he said. That's what the man said.

### Notes

1. Paul Tournier, *Guilt and Grace: A Psychological Study,* trans. Arthur W. Heathcote, J. J. Henry, and P. J. Allcock (New York: Harper, 1962), 67. Translation of *Vraie ou fausse culpabilité.*
2. William Klassen, *The Forgiving Community* (Philadelphia: Westminster, 1966), 45.

## 7

# WHO FORGIVES WHOM IN MARRIAGE?

No, I will not forgive you," the husband said. "Oh, no."

"I never intended to have an affair," she explained. "I blundered into it when I went back to college. Here at home alone all day, with the children both away at the university, I was so lonely, so empty. When I went back to do my master's, I found people I liked. I tried to talk with you about my new circle of friends, but you were busy. And I was getting farther and farther away from you. When I started doing the joint research project with Ray, I got emotionally involved. I knew I was wrong, but I was angry at you, and your job, and all the time you spent away. I realize now how cheap it was to get even in this way. I am so sorry. Someday, I hope there can be forgiveness."

"I hope so, too," the man replied. "I'm so confused and angry and hurt and guilty all at the same time I don't know what I really feel or want right now. But I do know that I'm hoping, somehow, we can find some kind of forgiveness."

"You do? But you just said—"

"I just said I won't forgive you, and I also said I hope there will be forgiveness between us."

"I don't understand."

"The last thing I want is for me to forgive you, as if I were totally in the right, and you were the sole wrongdoer. No, I'm afraid of what that would do to us both for the rest of our lives. I want to find out what my part was in all this. Maybe then we can forgive each other."

"You do want forgiveness?"

"Yes, but not the kind my sister gave to her husband. He's been paying through the nose ever since. I want to work through whatever it is between us and see if we can't begin again."

❧   ❧   ❧

Forgiveness in marriage is rarely a simple one-way matter. It takes two to have a problem; people don't have problems alone. More often responsibility lies somewhere between the partners rather than at either doorstep. People who marry each other are drawn together by similarities too deep for either to recognize. They may be attracted by their surface differences and superficial similarities, but at the core there are profound similarities that bond them to one another and blind them to much that is taking place between them. Differences are the occasion for our difficulties, but similarities are the deeper cause.

There are two false myths about responsibility.

*Myth one—that one person can be totally to blame and the other innocent.* In truth, there is always shared responsibility for what happens in a marriage relationship; it is never totally one-sided or it would never have been a marriage.

*Myth two—that responsibility, or "blame," is always fifty-fifty.* This is equal nonsense with the first. There are always ratios of responsibility, differences in degree of failure of the other and of the covenant. In an abusive marriage, for example, it may be ninety-ten. In the case of mental illness, ratios and the fixing of responsibility become totally irrelevant and irresponsible. There is such a thing as moral inability; and recognizing the differences in capacity to choose, act, and relate responsibly becomes a totally different set of concerns.

Forgiveness in marriage, regardless of responsibility for the injury done, must be two-way, or it will not continue to be a marriage; and it will be two-way or it will not be forgiveness at all. Instead, it often becomes a covert strategy for expressing judgment, perhaps condemnation, that may alienate the two forever after.

Sometimes the most destructive thing one can do in a relationship is to "forgive" the other person. When authentic forgiveness happens, both are changed, both come to meet the other, both pledge to work at reconstructing the relationship, both seek to give and receive genuine repentance for whatever has happened.

The righteous anger of the one party must be surrendered along with the defensive anger of the other. Both share in creating the relationship that allowed, perhaps invited, the hurts that have arisen. Both must journey across the distance that divides them if they are to truly meet. Reconciliation comes when there is mutual openness and mutual willingness to change. This is what the Bible refers to as mutual submission. It is a mutual caring—a mutual concern for the other's welfare.

## The Atmosphere of Forgiving

The marriage relationship that welcomes reconciliation of differences, renegotiation of understandings, and reconstructing of relationships has an atmosphere of liberating love. This freedom of forgiveness is something that must be felt to be fully appreciated. Each sets the other free to live spontaneously, to live joyfully and fully, to live with an honest openness and an open honesty.

The normal Western family does not allow such freedom. Most families handle their differences by not talking about them, avoid their conflicts by denying that they exist, and bury their problems under a surface of niceness. (For one who loves honesty and genuineness, life with chronically nice, even terminally nice, people is cloying. At times one prays, "Please God, not one more cheerful person today. Could I have just one who is real?")

This atmosphere of avoidance and denial, maintained out of peace-loving motives, requires a blindness to injustice, a deafness to feelings, and an insensitivity to the hurts of relationship. Jesus once described the conspiracy of silence among good people in startling words:

> [He] who hath ears to hear, let him hear. . . . they seeing see not; and hearing they hear not, neither do they understand. . . . By hearing ye shall hear and shall not understand; and seeing ye shall see, and shall

not perceive: For [the] heart is waxed gross, [the] ears are dull of hearing, [the] eyes [are] closed; lest at any time they should see with their eyes, and hear with their ears, and should understand with their heart, and should [turn and change and be healed] (Matthew 13:9, 13–15 KJV)

## Five Basic Freedoms

The atmosphere of freedom, to both fail and succeed—to be human—is central to love for the other person. If one loves only the successful, appreciates only the beautiful, cares only for another when the other is performing, complying, and achieving, then there is no real love at all. Love sets the other free to be human. It cancels conditions and accepts the other with as few reservations as is humanly possible.

The five freedoms visible in such an atmosphere of marital acceptance and unconditional familial love are basic rights that go with the territory of personhood—they are as essential to being a fully alive and aware human being as is breathing. These are inalienable freedoms in family life, but freedoms that are often denied in the name of love when love is confused with control. When they are respected, the person feels and knows in the gut that he is precious, that she is prized, that he is valued with equal regard.

1. *The freedom to see what one sees.* Love sets us free to see what is; the old denial process demands that we live by silent "loyalties" that bind and blind. The more I love you, the more I set you free. The more I feel obligated to "loyalty," the more I must refuse to see what is, deny what was, and avoid what might be. So I rewrite the past, read out threats, read in fantasies. Our life together becomes a charade, a pretense, a mime.

The family that keeps faith sets each person free to see—see with his own eyes what his eyes see.

2. *The freedom to think one's own thoughts.* Respect invites each person to think his own thoughts. "Obligations" pressure a person to repeat others' ideas without making them his own, to replicate others' lives without understanding, to be a recorded announcement with an identity that is secondhand.

The family that respects persons invites each person to think—to think her own thoughts as a responsible thinker.

3. *The freedom to feel one's own feelings.* Caring sets another free to

feel, to feel positive and negative emotions, to own irritation and affection. Fear intimidates one to suppress feelings, repress excitement, and depress hopes of being fully present with others. So the senses are dulled, feelings are cut off, and people become superficial, surface, saintly, and safe.

The family that cares for persons frees them to feel—feel their own feelings, own them as their own, and know them as rich emotional energies by which they experience their perceptions and interactions.

4. *The freedom to choose what one wants.* Valuing another is honoring the freedom to respond voluntarily, choose with integrity, will with inner direction, and want what one truly wants. Shame coerces one to submit blindly to outer direction, to yield the will in self-doubt, to yield up the privilege of personhood.

The family that values another values voluntary response—each member becomes a responder, not a reactor, capable of responding freely, not forced to react automatically.

5. *The freedom to act—to speak, to risk, and to be real.* Prizing another is delighting in that person's freedom to act as a responsible being, to speak as a real person of integrity, to risk living as a genuine person working out full fidelity with self, with others, and with God. Selflessness leads us to be copies of others, conforming to patterns that are not our own acts of centered commitment.

The family that prizes each other prizes integrity. It prizes the right of each to act from a center that is the integer—the integrating core, the solid sense of selfhood—in relationship with all others.

When partners in a marriage are free to see reality, think with honesty, feel with integrity, choose responsibly, and act maturely, they create an atmosphere that invites children to mature fully. The two central internal functions of a healthy marriage are to create a union that nurtures both partners to wholeness and to create healthy children. A good marriage has an outer focus as well, in service and caring for the world about them.

In such family living, perfection is no longer seen as required; but maturity is prized. Conformity is no longer coerced; responsibility is valued. Failure is not feared; forgiveness is practiced.

Since most persons grow up in families that are less than open, genuine, warm, caring, and free in the ways we have been describing, it is the norm for marriages to struggle through repeated times of severe stress. Healthy marriages do not avoid such stressful times; they recognize, welcome, and work through them. They recognize that the passage between one stage of life and the next may be stormy; yet the weathering of the tempest is what gives life depth, and forgiveness is what provides the richness that infuses life with grace.

For many couples, accepting the help of others in the Christian community is a great source of support, whether this comes from other couples, from a pastor, or from a person trained in marriage counseling.

Most of us quickly see a dentist when a tooth aches, a mechanic when the car breaks down, or a doctor when pain strikes. Why not get help when marriage gets stormy?

What are the danger signals?

### Increasing Distance

The first danger signal is an increase in distance between two partners. Check to see if you are retreating from your problems instead of resolving them, allowing distance to prevent you from finding forgiveness.

The frustrations of daily living with another human being can turn into agendas for changing the other or—if one learns the obvious truth that one cannot change another for more than three days—they can offer a suggestion list for changes in the self. (Self-change is the only change that is permanent.) Maturity comes when we give up fantasies of changing the partner and forget the romantic propaganda that insists, "A happy marriage has no conflicts, no problems, no irritating disagreements—there can be no anger." If such marriages are made in heaven, they apparently stay there. They rarely appear on earth.

Any marriage will have problems, because normal growth creates new situations, with new demands that require new understandings. So of course there are conflicts. Misunderstanding is inevitable. Disagreements are unavoidable. Anger is always possible. Destructive anger distances; it erects walls of self-protection guarded by threats of further injury to the relationship or the other. Constructive anger attacks the barriers, the walls, the obstacles to relating and does not attack the other person. It seeks ways across the fault lines that open between partners, ways to bridge the gaps, ways to tear down protective walls that get hastily built and then passionately maintained.

A marriage—like every living thing—is in constant danger of deterioration. It also offers the possibility of continuing growth and maturation. And that's a task for both parties. There must be a mutual involvement in resolving the tensions and conflicts that arise. Creating an atmosphere of forgiveness and acceptance is the primary agenda for Christian marriage.

## Loss of Communication

The second danger signal is loss of communication. Any marriage can go through periods or may reach the point where the two just can't communicate, and both freeze into uncomfortable and unyielding silences, broken only by hostile words or ironical digs as irritation replaces affection.

To restore open communication, the first task is to listen. Listening is 90 percent of good communication. It's not just "the other half of talking." It's a skill—one that must be learned and practiced—all the time. Most people find it hard even to listen half the time, and then only with half of the mind.

Genuine, attentive listening has become so unusual that finding a good listener almost makes you lose your train of thought. It's like the wife whose husband dropped his newspaper and turned full attention on her. "Stop it," she snapped. "You're deliberately listening just to confuse me."

Actually, to listen is the queen of compliments; to ignore, the chief of insults. To become human, everyone needs listeners; and to be human, each must learn to listen.

A quick checklist on basic listening skills includes the following:

- Do you listen with your eyes as well as your ears? Or do your eyes stray and betray your wandering interests? (A good listener listens with all the senses.)
- Do you let the other's words and ideas fly by while you plan your next comment, consider your objection, explore the next topic you hope to interject, or cook up some sage word with which to stun the other at the first opportunity?
- Do you interrupt others or, even worse, second-guess them, trying to finish their statements or coaching them when they stumble or search for a word?

- Do you probe, question, interrogate, and cross-examine, thus dominating the conversation or perhaps revealing impatience or suggesting some feeling of superiority?
- Or do you truly listen? Can you go beyond merely hearing words and phrases to catch the ideas? And beyond the ideas to the feelings? Beyond the expressions to the true intent? Beneath the informational surface to the relational depth? Beyond the report to the rapport?

Love is a warm listener! Have you ever talked with someone who listened with such abandon and attention to what you were trying to say that it drew you out? Called forth your best? Even helped to clarify your thoughts by the very quality of their attending? Or have you started out to vent frustration or offer a few complaints about circumstances, but your friend's understanding love given in complete attention made you see things in a new light, and instead of inviting sympathy you clarified your problem?

Remember when you were involved in a personal tragedy? Did you want someone to talk to you? Give you an appropriate word of sympathy? Or a little sermonette of encouragement? No, you wanted someone who loved you enough to sit patiently and listen to your feelings, to give understanding and acceptance of you and the pain you were facing.

In a time of pain, nothing is more ineffective than offering a speech of comfort and counsel that advises one to "keep a stiff upper lip, look on the bright side—after all it might have been worse, every cloud has a silver lining, and it will all work out for the best."

I recall with puzzlement a time of serious loss in my life when I needed help and turned to a minister friend to share my suffering. After three sentences, he interrupted to give me a flawlessly worded, lovely speech of comfort and encouragement. But the farther he went, the more distant it became. I wanted to reach out, grasp his lapel, and say, "Come back. I don't want a bouquet of words. I want you!"

I can remember with similar pain a moment when I too gave a friend in need the stone of eloquent comfort when what was wanted was the bread of human understanding. No matter how polished, perfect, and multifaceted the precious stone I offered, it provided no nourishment. He couldn't eat diamonds—even if they are "forever."

Once you have been on the receiving end, such moments of pain call out something different from you—empathy, compassion, and silence. In such moments, the only love wanted is called listening.

Caring is hearing. Love is the opening of your life to another in listening, compassionate understanding, and honest sharing. An open ear is the only believable sign of an open heart. You learn to understand life—you learn to *live*—as you learn to listen. To love your neighbor is to listen as you listen to yourself. The Golden Rule of friendship is to listen to others as you would have them listen to you.

Communication in marriage begins with listening. It grows with genuine understanding. For a husband and wife, being understanding is the crucial step toward being the right mate. Whether or not you found "the right mate" is not the important thing for happiness in marriage. The crucial step is your willingness to be the right person to your partner.

In his book *To Understand Each Other,* Paul Tournier points out that when a husband complains, "But she doesn't understand me," or "I just can't understand that woman," he is only saying in shorthand, "I don't think she accepts me," or "I can't accept my wife." But the commitment to be understanding, loving, and accepting can begin to change all that.[1]

## Negative Spirals of Reactivity

The positive spirals of affection expressed in confirmation that is voiced in repeated affirmations that are received as validations which return to deepened affection become a continuous feeling loop. The spiral becomes an interlocking series of signals of caring that connects the two; supplies soothing when there is stress, irritation, or fatigue; and provides relationship repair when there are misunderstandings. These are positive spirals of response.

The negative spirals are equally familiar. They are composed of criticism, coldness, contempt, silent stonewalling, withdrawal, and distancing. These interlocking emotions and actions cluster and breed like an infection that inflames irritability and rots away the relational tie. The couple needs to balance any occurrence of these elements by interrupting the spiral and returning to repair-responses—apology, validation of the other, and a resumption of the positive spiral of mutual confirmation of the other's preciousness and exclusive importance.

## Growing Resentment

The fourth danger signal comes when the attitudes or actions of the other begin to irritate, alienate, and accumulate. Taking them along to bed at night, refusing to make up, and letting "the sun go down upon your wrath" (Ephesians 4:26 KJV) foster a stone wall of silent resentment.

After a few years of marriage, nonverbal communication becomes an increasingly trusted way of reading the other's responses. It is sometimes unerringly accurate—the mouth may lie, but the body will invariably tell the truth. Reading the other's signals may offer a clear understanding of his or her level of presence or interest, but it is powerless to solve problems.

Misunderstanding and miscommunication can only be resolved by an effort to discuss it and talk it out. Openness is the language of love. Love is the opening of your life to another, the trust that lays life bare to another.

Such trust is possible where people frequently reaffirm their pledge of faithful loyalty. True loyalty is a pledge of unconditional allegiance to one another in thoughts, plans, actions, and attitudes. It is a pledge that must be demonstrated in full acceptance of the other in an until-death-do-us-part contract.

Loyalty is a matter of priorities. And a husband-wife promise of love is by very nature an exclusive promise that eliminates all competition. He or she comes first and knows it! That assurance of first loyalty is the source of true security.

We all crave the security that comes from belonging to someone who loves us in return for our love. We long for the joy we can feel when we are bringing happiness to someone we love. We need the security that intimacy, open honesty, and acceptance give. And security is possible only where there is fidelity. Unity, loyalty, and security are totally dependent on fidelity to each other.

The late Swiss theologian Emil Brunner once wrote, "Marriage is based not so much on love as on fidelity." Fidelity is allegiance with no reservations, no hesitation. It is more than fidelity in sexuality. It is being faithful in thought as well as act, faithful in fulfilling the deep emotional and spiritual needs of the other, and faithful in solving or resolving the inevitable misunderstandings and conflicts. Such a marriage is only possible when it is cemented and recemented by forgiving love.

The husband and wife who discover the deepest levels of intimacy are those who give each other the completely unconditional acceptance of depth-forgiveness. They reach toward total forgiveness, knowing that it brings a unity that is truly complementary and completing.

## Reversing the Spirals That Spin Us

The secrets of reversing old spirals that spin us out of control and, for the moment, threaten the marriage with the possibility that we might crash and burn, are, like all useful secrets, present already in your marriage. If the relationship has enough emotional investment to foul itself up with passion, it also has the power within it to create positive change.

There are no general rules that always succeed in enabling couples to resolve differences without hurting each other, but there are several ground rules that can offer ways of resolving things creatively with each other. (These are guides for essentially healthy marriages—ways to make a good marriage better. They are not paths that should be followed in marriages that are locked in dominant-submissive patterns, or principles that should be exaggerated by persons caught up in controlling, violating, or violent relationships.)

1. *Define what the difference—the conflict—is about.* Studies on conflict in marriage show that in about three-fourths of the conflicts, the spouses are fighting about different issues. He is ticked at something she said or did today; she is losing it because of something he did two weeks ago. Define the difference together—and define it in normal, natural, neutral language. Define it narrowly, mutually, jointly, and you can better find a solution together.

2. *Stand together against the problem, not against each other, seeing the other as the problem.* It's not me versus you, it's me and you versus the problem. It's silly to try to win over the other, stupid to try to make the other lose. No one wins unless both win. If either loses, his or her second thought is to seek a rematch. Many marriages may once

have been a "match made in heaven" but became a rematch of a rematch of a rematch of many previous rematches.

3. *Listen actively, accurately, and caringly.* Reverse the attitude:"When I talk, she/he listens," to " When I listen, she/he talks to me." Or "When I am heard, I feel loved," to "When I can hear the other deeply, I feel an atmospheric change from fear to love."

4. *Always seek to make the other look good, feel good about himself, feel good about the outcome of the conflict, and feel good about being in a deeply honest relationship with you.* Making the other feel bad about himself will make him feel bad about you, your marriage, and your life together.

5. *Develop a short memory.* When you bury the hatchet, do not insist on remembering exactly where it was buried—in case you need it in the future. When you end a difficult interaction, truly bring it to an end. When you let go of a grievance, let go of the arguments, the rationale for your position, and the winning arguments that could be saved for the next round.

6. *When an issue arises, make a mental list of all the things that link you to* balance *over against the item that* separates you; *when a* bad thing *bugs you, see it in relation to the* good things *that connect you.* Always begin to work on a difference from the point where your relationship is the strongest, not from the spot where it is the weakest. Build on the healthy parts of your trust and respect, not on the troubled parts.

7. *Disarm your heart.* You cannot get at the negativity in another without getting it out of your own soul. I cannot eliminate the irritation in our relationship without first limiting it in my relating to you. We love disarmingly by disarming our love.

### Note

1. From Paul Tournier, *To Understand Each Other,* trans. John S. Gilmour (Atlanta, Ga.: John Knox, 1981; Louisville, Ky.: Westminster John Knox, 1967, 1988), 21–22. Translation of *Difficultés Conjugales.*

# 8

# HOW DOES FORGIVENESS CHALLENGE PREJUDICE?

He's bigoted.

She's prejudiced.

I have principles.

What is your metaphor for *prejudice?* The metaphor one uses to explain or excuse one's prejudices is the most significant clue to how he or she deals with this chronic human parasite. *Parasite* is a metaphor of infection, like a virus in the computer—a foreign invasion that avoids responsibility for the intruder.

The lightest of metaphors—the one used most commonly to explain such feelings to ourselves—is that it's simply a matter of *personal taste*. Everyone has his own personal set of preferences—some people discriminate against cats, others dislike oysters; there are even those who reject chocolate. It's all a matter of taste, preference, perhaps allergy—and there is no debating taste. The metaphor of taste is for most persons their unconscious self-defense's preferred image. There is nothing as toxic as a bad metaphor, and a metaphor that excuses one as easily as this should be a bit suspect as a slick escape from responsibility for attitudes that have profound and disturbing—often violent—consequences.

Consider an alternate metaphor—prejudice as a *trial*. Imagine a courtroom, a judical proceeding. The hearing is in its final hours. After days of prosecution, finally the defense is to be heard. Day after day witnesses have amassed evidence.

At last the case for the defense. But wait! Where is the jury? What! Gone out for coffee? And the judge? He's nodding at his desk! The defense is being presented, but no one is there to hear.

And *you* are the defendant. It's your trial. You are on trial for your life, without defense. No one will hear your side of the case. No one cares.

Now you realize you were judged before the trial began, sentenced before the evidence was heard, condemned without mercy—before you ever came to court.

What if that were you! What if you were judged without opportunity of reply and condemned for false reasons mouthed by false witnesses in a false trial? What if you were prejudged—by others' prejudices? What if it happened to you?

Does this offer a more accurate metaphor for our prejudices about class, race, religion, gender, age, ethnic origin, or any other category we use to classify others? Does it fit the way we label, stereotype, rank in importance, dismiss, criticize, or condemn without hearing the case for the defense? Every time you hear a prejudicial statement, make a prejudicial judgment, or laugh at a bit of prejudicial merriment, does this metaphor become a reality?

## Principle One: Things Perceived to Be Real Are Real in Their Consequences

False as the judgment about a group may be, when it is perceived to be real, it has real consequences. Unsubstantiated as a belief about another race indeed is, when it is believed, it has real effects. Spurious as a conviction about the other gender, the differing neighbor, or the person from another class truly is, it does shape our responses, affect our votes, and alter our contribution to the larger community atmosphere.

Prejudice is "prejudging"—weighing another's worth with your thumb on the scales, screening the other's viewpoint with blinders on your eyes. Prejudice is passing a judgment of discrimination against others on the basis of things they did not cause, could not change, and should not regret. The process is not a logical, reasonable, rational, or responsible use of our basic human capacities.

Prejudice answers to none of these. It is an emotion become a conviction, a suspicion become a certainty, a question turned into its own answer. When we speak of *prejudices* we say, "I feel." When we speak of *opinions* we say, "I think." When we speak of *convictions* we say, "I know!" You may challenge convictions with logic or change opinions by argument. But not prejudices. They answer to no outside authority. They are nonverbal reactions to internalized images, unaware reflex responses to buried metaphors we seldom realize we possess.

### Principle Two: Prejudice Is a Denied, Excused, and Dangerous Mental Disorder

Prejudice is not simply a poor social judgment, a personal foible, or an excusable bias that is a quaint quirk of some persons or personalities. It is a serious mental illness. It can be diagnosed, defined, and named as a mental disorder which judges, alienates, devalues, distances, denigrates, discriminates, and ultimately destroys humanness and human community.

In 1921—observe, *1921*— in Topeka, Kansas, Dr. Karl Menninger, the most respected American psychiatrist of his generation, declared to the hospital staff he administered that there would be no further discrimination on the basis of race or social class tolerated in any and all decisions made on the campus. "Anyone who objects can either resign immediately or submit themselves for treatment, because prejudice is a form of mental illness."

Prejudice, like all other mental illnesses, has components that are learned from the values of the family and community, where one is taught the contents and objects of prejudice. And there are components that are caught—like all other diseases. It is an illness—a character disease that is transmitted as easily and accidentally as any physical sickness from contact with trusted models, respected authority figures, influential peers, and the malaise or mind-set of the general public.

You and I are infected. We are all prejudiced. What's worse, we are carriers. Our children catch it from us as they "catch on" to the hidden meanings of our uncaring words or unfeeling jokes. Any slip of the tongue, innocent as it may seem, transmits the fetid contents of a diseased spot festering in the dark recesses of the unconscious. (Does this sound overly dramatic? It is clinically accurate.) The so-called incidental remark then transfers the contagion to another, and within a short time it replicates the unhealthy attitudes that guarantee the development of whole colonies of prejudice.

Who of us truly knows what lies hidden in the depths of the mind? We may not be responsible for all the prejudices assimilated during maturing years, but if they are still in use, or one is still used by them as a host or carrier, then for that, one is fully responsible. Once society winked at snobbish feelings of superiority, but there is no room in our shrinking world for prejudice.

If you sometimes have the thought that you're superior to any other because your skin is white, or pink, or tan, cancel it decisively. Such prejudices have no basis in mentally healthy thinking. They have been long ago disproved, and it's high time they were despised and discarded.

There is a way to find release from your prejudices. There is a way for you, whether you are a Christian in a white, Anglo-Saxon Protestant church; a not-yet-Christian wondering if faith in Christ can make any difference; or an indeed-I'm-not-a-Christian pointing out the uncomfortable fact that 11:00 A.M. on Sunday is still the most segregated hour of the week.

Consider the one absolutely unprejudiced Man who ever lived, the one person who offered personal, social, spiritual, and moral help in conquering prejudice—Jesus Christ!

"Now wait," you may say, "the followers of Christ are among the most prejudiced people in our nation." Yes, some of them are. Harvard psychologist Gordon Allport, in his book *The Nature of Prejudice,* wrote, "The role of religion is paradoxical. It makes prejudice and it unmakes prejudice. . . . Churchgoers are more prejudiced than the average; they are also less prejudiced than the average."[1]

Why this polarity, this vast difference? Why does religion make some people bigoted and intolerant but others more understanding, caring, and accepting? Repeated research on this issue reveals a consistent set of findings. Those whose religious experience is extrinsic—simply a social, casual, semihabitual participation in religious practice that is not internalized into values and assimilated into the deep rituals of their lives—end up being more prejudiced than nonreligious persons. Those persons whose religious experience is intrinsic experience

—an individual, intensely personal, deeply value-oriented faith that is internalized in life and practice—show a significant decrease in prejudice in contrast to all other groups.

Thus, those persons who *use* religion—for status, security, or social opportunity—seem from all research findings to accept only the parts of religion that reinforce their own views. But those persons who allow the faith-values of love for neighbor that are central to all the ethical systems of the major religions to truly shape their lives find that this weakens the mental illness of prejudice—person-directed hatred.

Those persons who find in a deeply internalized faith the centering values that order their lives by transcendent ethical and universal moral convictions find that it is possible to love their neighbors. The new pattern, such as that seen in Christ, redefines for them what it means to be a human being to fellow humans and a child of God to all God's other children. Can it be that as they die to prejudice, they are born again to a life of love, as Christ promised they would?

Choosing a life-organizing model such as Jesus lifts one's value orientation out of a social context that fosters the growth of the viruses of hate and prejudice. Reflection on Christ's life reveals an alternative.

➣ ➣ ➣

He was born in the most rigidly ethnic culture of all time; was born in a fiercely nationalistic nation; was reared in Galilee, the most bigoted, backwoods area of that nation; was born into a family of snobbish royal lineage; was born in a time when revolutionary fanaticism fired every heart with hatred for the Roman oppressors; was born in a country practicing the apartheid of rigid segregation between Jews and Samaritans. Yet He consistently confronted and often ridiculed any trace of bigotry.

He taught, "Love your neighbor as yourself," which means, according to the best commentators, "Love your neighbor, for he is like you, for she is the same as you." He lived it.

"Greater love hath no man than this," He once said, "that a man lay down his life for his friends" (John 15:13 KJV). He did it.

He summed up His goals in life with these words: "The Spirit of the Lord is on me, because he has anointed me to preach good news to the poor. He has sent me to proclaim freedom for the prisoners and recovery of sight for the blind, to release the oppressed, [to announce that this is the year of celebrating and observing the jubilee of the Lord's loving generosity]" (Luke 4:18–19 NIV).

And when he became the victim of a nation's prejudicial fear and frozen rage at such integrity, He did all that He had taught. He died for it. He died as the victim of prejudicial hatreds, was sentenced at a trial without defense, was condemned by those who had prejudged Him, was abused and beaten in fulfillment of human prejudices, and was executed as the innocent victim of His peers.

⟩⟩　　⟩⟩　　⟩⟩

Those who wish to stand on the side of Jesus Christ will need to reject prejudice whenever, however, and wherever they find it. In themselves, first of all; then, and only then, in the world about them.

What will this mean? *The first step: Make friends across racial lines.* Why should you have only white (or black, or brown, or yellow) friends? Why advance the cause of prejudice by limiting your friendships to "your kind"?

This will mean going where the barriers are. Refuse to go to a one-race-only church. Avoid restaurants and businesses that cater to only one kind of people. Welcome families of other races to move into your block. If you employ, hire on the basis of actual qualifications only, not on the basis of phony fears of color problems.

If you say you love your neighbor, live it—as Jesus did—without prejudging your neighbor by your prejudices.

All of this is the first step toward the open acceptance of others that is so basic to the forgiving style of life.

*The second step: Stop judging by your biases.* This is an even more subtle temptation. It's the habit we often consider an asset, whereas it may be our greatest liability. It's the automatic reflex of judging others that takes place as we label—and libel—all those around us.

The use of labels is the undeniable sign of a judgmental mindset. One might never say, "Look, it's obvious that the guy's subversive; he's a Communist." Or was it, "Listen, that fellow's such a conservative—such an extremist—he's got two right hands."? The use of labels places the other in a despised or demeaned category without attending to the unique value of the person.

From the first childhood labels to the more sophisticated adult classifications, all that's changed is the vocabulary. The mentality is the same, and so is the effect. Words are wonderful things as long as they are symbols for thought. But once you convert your words from symbols to labels, they replace thought.

Labels are not only signs of mental stagnation in the *user*, they are also unhealthy for the *person labeled*.

Labels are libels because they are irrational and illogical. Any textbook on elementary logic begins by demanding that you discard your labels and paste pot because "labels are the most common and foolish logical fallacy." And they are. A label is a weasel word. It's as two-faced or as many-faced as there are users and hearers.

Labels are libels because of their inherent dishonesty. Politicians use them to smear opponents, debaters employ them to brace up weak arguments, and shallow thinkers use them to pretend intelligence.

Well, that's all true, but that's how *others* use labels; that's not what you or I do! *We* use labels because they're handy things for sorting out people. A people-watcher has got to have various classifications, and names and labels too, if he or she is going to make some sense out of the human race—right?

And yet, that's exactly where labels shortchange us most. When we use them as cubbyhole categories, nice little shelves where we stick people for good, we think we've got solid information on hand—but we don't. "I've got his number," we say. "He's one of that kind." But you can't simplify people like that! Labelers believe that the world is contained by their categories.

There are only two kinds of people in the world—those who think there are two kinds, and those who think there are more. To this proverb, theologian John Howard Yoder used to add, "There are only two kinds of people on earth: the good and the bad. And the good decide which are which."

That's getting at the root of the problem. Those who believe that they are good enough to criticize others and place them into their proper categories are good—in their own eyes. So good people go on and on, pigeonholing each other under "appropriate" labels and closing the door to understanding, acceptance, friendship, and brotherly love. This is the sort of goodness we can all do without. It's a small-minded goodness. As the common proverb says (labeling behavior, not persons), "Great minds discuss ideals; average minds discuss events; small minds discuss people."

Habitual labeling, like chronic critical attitudes, is actually a symptom of emotional disturbance. The knocker, complainer, belittler, or gossiper suffers from a variety of the mental disorder of prejudice compounded by the sin of malice.

People who stir up trouble are generally troubled people. They pick at others to salve their own feelings of guilt by pointing out others who are worse than they; or to reduce the pressures of jealousy by ventilating about another's weaknesses; or to scapegoat others for faults they find difficult to own up to in themselves; or to ease emotional tension and frustration within their own personalities; or to fulfill their own wishes and desires in imagination, since they cannot or will not do them in act.

*True or false:* Have you ever criticized another's fault, then discovered that it was your own fault too, but felt a bit justified for your own failure or frustration? Then feel at home in the human race.

*True or false:* Did you ever react to a situation in which you didn't get what you want, or lost what you prized? And so you critiqued innocent but irritating people who stood in the way? Or passed the buck for your misfortune to some third party?

*True or false:* Do you ever criticize in order to eliminate competition or to climb toward your ambition? Do you ever wish misfortune on enemies, competitors, or persons who threaten your success? Do you let your gossip trample on those who get in your way? Do you belittle those beneath you to win approval of those above you?

*True or false:* Do you ever find that when you criticize another's failure it serves to reduce guilt feelings about a similar shortcoming in yourself—or the desire for it—or to minimize your own guilt and responsibility? Do you conform to the majority against your better knowledge, and then gossip and criticize the minority whose honest stand made you feel guilty? Do you habitually pick on those who get caught for doing what you get away with?

You can grade yourself on this test, just so you know the score. Does it tend to verify your suspicion that your interest in nit-picking others has emotional roots? That chronic criticism is only a symptom of much deeper problems?

An astute critic of human behavior, Jesus, One who criticized with the same integrity with which he lived, said these words about criticism:

"Don't criticize people, and you will not be criticized. For you will be judged by the way you criticize others, and the measure you give will be the measure you receive.

"Why do you look at the speck of sawdust in your brother's eye and fail to notice the plank in your own? How can you say to your brother, 'Let me get the speck out of your eye,' when there is a plank in your own? You fraud! Take the plank out of your own eye first, and then you can see clearly enough to remove your brother's speck of dust." (Matthew 7:1–5)

Commenting on these words of Christ, William Barclay suggests three great reasons why no one can judge another. (1) "We never know the whole facts or the whole person." We cannot understand the circumstances or temptations. (2) "It is almost impossible for any [one] to be strictly impartial in judgment." (3) "No [one] is good enough to judge any other [person]." Our own faults and our own inability to resolve them automatically disqualify us as fair critics.[2]

First, we may note in summary, if we seek to live in the love that is the prerequisite to all forgiving, we will rarely judge and criticize. That is so because when one views others with the acceptance that restores the perception of the other person's preciousness and sees them with understanding eyes in as far as this is within the realm of human possibility, then any critique is first evaluated according to its purpose. Is it for the purpose of helping, lifting, and redeeming? Or is it for the purpose of punishing or getting even?

Second, it is evaluated in light of one's own situation—admitting where we too are guilty of the same fault and dealing first with ourselves before we proceed to others. Frequently, the criticism is dismissed at this point. Once we reflect on the fact that our own life is open to the scrutiny of the Judge of all the earth, the plank of a malicious or vengeful spirit is in part withdrawn. Then we can see our way clear to remove the splinter in the other's eye.

The prerequisite love (accepting others as persons, treating them as fellow human beings in need of the mercy and love of God) demonstrates the willingness to seek the reconciliation that is greater than any need to offer criticism. It affirms and extends the loving, understanding, forgiving help of one all-too-human human being to another.

In a context of authentic equal regard for the other, relationship is reaffirmed and personal dignity is recognized. Then conversation about differences, injuries, or conflicts can be invited with few internal conflicts breaking out to stir up conflict within the other and without creating the kind of differences between persons that ignites the conflict within each person into a common fire.

ᠵ    ᠵ    ᠵ

Thomas Merton, one of this generation's best writers and careful thinkers about spirituality, tells of a transforming moment that happened in downtown Louisville that was a turning point in his life. Merton was a brilliant man, a graduate of schools in England, France, and America who had a marvelous sense of humor with a dark side of biting sarcasm.

His tendency to look down on others with a snobbish superiority was little changed by his conversion to Christianity, his entrance into the priesthood, and his becoming a member of the Trappist monastic community. After many years as a monk, much of it spent in solitary meditation, this intense experience of reverence for God's presence in the very people he habitually viewed with condescension broke through the patterns of discrimination.

> In Louisville, at the corner of Fourth and Walnut, in the centre of the shopping district, I was suddenly overwhelmed by the realization that I loved all those people, that they were mine and I theirs, that we could not be alien to one another even though we were total strangers. It was like waking from a dream of separateness, of spurious self-isolation in a special world, the world of renunciation and supposed holiness. . . .
>
> This sense of liberation from an illusory difference was such a relief and such a joy to me that I almost laughed out loud. . . .
>
> It is a glorious destiny to be a member of the human race, though it is a race dedicated to many absurdities and one which makes many terrible mistakes: yet, with all that, God Himself gloried in becoming a member of the human race. A member of the human race! To think that such a commonplace realization should suddenly seem like news that one holds the winning ticket in a cosmic sweepstake.
>
> . . . There is no way of telling people that they are all walking around shining like the sun.
>
> . . . If only we could see each other that way all the time. There would be no more war, no more hatred, no more cruelty, no more greed . . .
>
> . . . [The] gate of heaven is everywhere."[3]

From this moment forward, Merton's understanding turned from seeing Christianity as the love of ideas and principles, as he formerly believed, to the love of people—people who differ markedly from us, even our enemies. "It is my belief that we should not be too sure of having found Christ until we have found Him in that part of humanity that is most remote from our own."

## Notes

1. Gordon Allport, *The Nature of Prejudice* (Garden City: Doubleday, 1954), 143.
2. William Barclay, *The Gospel of Matthew, Vol. 1* (chapters 1–10 of Matthew), vol. 1 of The Daily Study Bible series, rev. ed. (Philadelphia: Westminster, 1975), 263–65.
3. Thomas Merton, *Conjectures of a Guilty Bystander* (New York: Doubleday, 1966), 140–42.

## 9

# IS FORGIVING
# A WAY OF
# EVERYDAY LIVING?

The waitress fumbled the plates of dessert, then dropped one across the shoulder of the guest of honor. The cake and lemon sauce spread a wide smear down his coat, tie, and shirt and ended in his lap.

In a few moments, this man, a United States senator, was to stand and speak to the five hundred guests of this prayer breakfast. Now he was trying with a dinner knife to lift off the gooey mess. The waitress returned with towels and tried in her embarrassment to help undo the slip of a hand.

The pained look on her face was not erased by the senator's murmuring, "It's OK. It'll be all right."

When the last bit of lemon sauce was wiped away, and she gathered her towels to go, the senator reached both hands to gently touch her face. He drew her down, and kissed her cheek. The blush faded. A smile took its place. She left the room, radiant, head erect, alive.

Watching this drama out of the corner of my eye, I suddenly saw—not what had just happened—but what he had actually done. He had taken a memory that would hurt painfully for the rest of her life, a memory that would arouse all the feelings of shame and guilt whenever it came back to her, and turned that memory into a story she would delight in telling. "Senator Harold Hughes kissed me right there just after I'd dropped a dessert—" she'd be able to say with pride.

What a thousand words of "I forgive you" could not do (they would likely have hurt even more), one gentle act of acceptance did perfectly.

For those close enough to see, this unself-conscious drama of acceptance had a greater impact than the one-thousand-word address that followed. His message told the story of a transformed life—his own. It was a powerful story of the senator's own pilgrimage from a personal tragedy of alcoholism to a life of healing and rich service.

But the simple kiss of forgiveness was even more powerful. He understood how words may only add to the shame and pain, but a gentle act of acceptance and forgiveness can restore the soul.

## The Power of the Nonverbal

What the person is and does speaks more than what he or she says. A simple act of love is far more eloquent and much more believable than words. It's a handclasp that says, "I want to be close again," or a gesture of inclusion or recognition that says, "You are important to me—I want your love and respect," or a clear sign of remorse or regret that says, "I'm sorry."

All of these may be better than an effusive apology. When one says the words *I forgive you,* they can be easily tainted with superiority. What seems a generous statement of release can in reality conceal a hidden accusation, a subtle judgment.

Since forgiveness is a decision about an act of wrongdoing, it inevitably contains a judgment because it is a choice of what to do about an offense. To say "I forgive you" is to say "I have been wronged; I recognize this as a fact; I am willing to accept the wrongdoing without revenge or resentment." That contains an accusation, a judgment, and a decision on consequences.

When both parties are involved in the offense (as is often the case), when both share some ratio of responsibility for the estrangement, then to say "I forgive you" is more than a bit self-righteous. Far better, perhaps, to say, "I want to be close again, to accept and be accepted," or, "to forgive and be forgiven." Forgiveness, surprisingly often, needs to be two-way. Mutual. Reciprocal.

Notice all the ways this is said in the Bible: "Forgive as you have been forgiven." "Forgive as freely as forgiveness has been given you." "Ask for forgiveness only in the measure you are willing to extend to others." "If you do not forgive another his trespasses, neither will you be forgiven." "Confront another in the awareness of your own weakness, in memory of your own like tendencies to fail or fall." "Love the other as you love yourself." "Respect your neighbor as you want to be respected."

Forgiveness is so frequently a two-way street that one is often tempted to drop the word *forgiveness* from our vocabulary, since it can be so paternalistic and reflect such a superior-to-inferior relationship. "Use the word *acceptance,*" one great theologian has counseled. "It is two-way; it is mutual; it has an honest humility about it."

And that is a central point in Jesus' teaching on love for others— seek to restore right relationships, knowing that you too need acceptance and forgiveness if you are to be in right relationship with God and humanity (read Matthew 18:21–35). And, as has been said, such acceptance is frequently expressed better with actions of love than with a thousand words. To explore how action, not diction, is the most powerful language of forgiveness in everyday life, we must look at cases such as the following.

## The Power of the Unaware Becoming Aware

*Case one:* He was born into a talented, highly competitive family: a brilliant father, creative mother, winning sisters, and strong, successful brothers, but he was simply average in ability. He achieved within the range of normal performance, winning no attention or recognition in academics, like his sister; or athletics, like his brother; or music and drama, like both siblings.

In another family he would have found a respected place as an average, normal, ordinary Mr. Everybody. But here it was impossible. There were his father's high expectations to deal with, and his mother's dreams, not to mention brother-sister pressures. University? "Absolutely necessary," said the rest of the family. "No," said the young man.

He tried a job, business entanglements, financial responsibilities, serious courtship—all as ways of escape. "No, no, no," said Dad.

Finally he played an angry trump card. Quick marriage by elopement. He settled down to his chosen life. Forgot his family. But he found no satisfaction. Now that he had what he had wanted, he discovered it wasn't what he wanted after all. And all the old drives to achieve, to win recognition, awoke within him. Business success? No possibility. Social prominence? No admission. That left him one outlet—his church. He poured himself into it. For the missing education, he substituted piety. Pious activity could win respect and acclaim. Pious concerns shared as prayer requests could eliminate competitors. Conspicuous good works performed with obvious humility could garner recognition.

Then, just as he was achieving social power and leadership roles, the recognition he sought began to slip through his fingers. So he drove in stakes defensively. He formed stronger convictions, increasing his conservatism and dogmatism. Soon he found himself in the middle of threatening rifts. An intense conflict erupted between those who supported him and those valiant for a competing truth. Next came charges, accusations, and bitterness.

Many who were near to him understood the battles waging within his heart and the parallel conflicts surrounding him, but all hesitated to approach him. Who could help him see his own inner hurts and how they were projected onto others? Who cared enough to reach out with the attention, affection, and acceptance he needed early enough while it could still be heard?

There was such a person. A man of deep feeling and intuition who was poor with words but great with friendships, fishing rods, and love. He understood that this man—who seemed so sure of his rightness, so superior in his goodness—was really fragile, afraid, and hurting behind the armor.

He took him fishing. They didn't catch many fish, but they talked and listened to each other for a whole day. The man hadn't had anyone hear him out for years, and he loved a good listener. By evening he had discovered that he needed to go and talk to the person he had been criticizing and accusing the most.

Our angler had played no angles. He had only been present and at times honestly reflective. He gave him stubborn man-to-man acceptance, and it came as cool water to a man with a deep thirst. He had been starved for attention, and, surprisingly, one day's worth gave him enough nourishment to begin conversation with someone he had feared.

What a thousand words could not do in storming defenses, one action did by slipping past the guards. And the man in the fortress came out with his armor down, and he and the other truly met.

## The Power of Recognition and Respect

*Case two:* He was born into a family of no wealth, no reputation, no respected position in the community—nobodies.

His brothers and sisters were underachievers—dropouts at grade eight or nine. His father worked only several months out of the year. His mother struggled to keep body and soul together, stretching what little they had, stitching up what they wore and, in general, working enough for two people.

Was it anger over his dad's negligence, their unnecessary poverty? Was it humiliation over the patronizing smiles of his peer group? Was it sheer frustration at his own destitute way of life? Whatever the reason, he was fired with a new strain of family traits.

He slugged his way through high school, making the highest grades but not becoming valedictorian (not well-rounded enough—besides, you know his family). Somehow he held two jobs—one after school, one on weekends. Then came his break into a small business of his own.

He had difficulties socially—seldom with the girl, almost always with the parents. Still, he persevered.

Then came marriage. Financial success. Business prominence. Community recognition by people who saw him as the man he had become. But among his old friends and in his church? There he was still the boy from that family, who grew up in that house, on that street.

So he began to voice criticisms about little things that went wrong, to push against boundaries that seemed arbitrary, to press against points in his church that seemed intolerable. Others who shared his feelings of dissatisfaction gathered around him. Tensions grew. The congregation began to divide. Rumors spread. Accusations broke into the open. Old sneers at his family surfaced and circulated again.

Did no one understand? Truth was not on trial; love was. It was not a conservative-liberal conflict or even the new versus the old. It was the "ins" against the "outs." The establishment versus the intruder.

Did no one come to give the honest acceptance, recognition,

and love needed or deserved? Was no one willing to see him for what he wanted to be, for what he had worked to become, for what he now was?

There was someone. This time it was a pastor who recognized that this man not only had gifts; he had a deep urgency to contribute to the life of the church and to its ministry in the community.

The pastor could have spent two years in weekly sessions of pastoral psychotherapy with this man to help him sort out the roots of his anger, the dynamics of his conflicts with others, and the mixed motives in his concerns about the church. It would all have been accurate, insightful, perhaps reconciling. It might have ended in forgiveness and healing. But he chose another way.

He invited the man to enter a two-year teacher-disciple contract and became a supportive mentor. He delegated ministry tasks suited to the man's gifts, outlined training experiences, went to seminars with him, and watched him grow. Halfway into the second year, the man sold his business and went to seminary. There conviction was sharpened into clarity of faith and urgency was tempered into resources of love and compassion to aid others in their growth. His life was transformed over a five-year period, and the ministry he now offers to others is a gift of God.

It was not what the pastor *said,* although there were many words of wisdom in what he offered. It was *who he was* and *what he did.* He gave attention. He was available. He embodied the acceptance and forgiveness the man needed. He gave him a second chance at life. The man had painted himself into a corner without exits. The pastor gave him a new beginning without a loss of face or an attack on his faith.

## The Power of Equal Regard

*Case three:* She was Ms. Average Citizen. Average home. Average education. Average wealth. Normal. Usual. Run-of-the-mill. Not that she was Ms. Nobody; she was Ms. Everybody. But now and again she felt a deep dissatisfaction. Not that she consciously decided in those times, *I'll throw my weight around a little.* No, it was just that she had to place the weight of her frustrations somewhere.

So she'd find herself involved in conversations that turned critical, in comments that became evaluative and expressed the unrest of the larger group. She could apply a little pressure to get something changed that truly needed change and in addition served to make her presence felt. She could point out some problem or oversight, find some fault to rub with salt—to show that even she knew better than that and to let those on top hear from the rest of humanity.

She could quote a few appropriate criticisms when frustrations needed to be brought out into the open. She could anonymously stir the troubled waters that lie beneath the surface of any group. Not maliciously, mind you, but out of the frustration of being a taken-for-granted bit of the social backwaters. And in her church, where the social machine often ran without much lubrication of love, her refusing to be a smoothly meshing cog in the machine generated friction—with both heat and wear. In this case, her frustrations went unnoticed, her needs unmet, and the church suffered.

Of all places, a church should have an abundance of persons who recognize needs in each other and seek to meet them. People who can pick up the pieces and piece them together into wholeness, one-ness, rightness, and unity—that's what the work of forgiving and reconciling is.

Did no one see her needs, feel her loneliness, or care about her inner struggles? No. She was avoided and labeled as someone who caused trouble and dissention, was ignored as an irritant and treated as unwanted in the community. And she felt the exclusion Her needs were for inclusion, not for control. But those in power, to whom control was everything, used their power to edge her out of the church. There was no acceptance available for the critic, no forgiveness for the one who broke through the denial.

## The Power of Peacemaking

"Happy are the peacemakers," Jesus once said, "because they are called God's sons" (see Matthew 5:9). Yes, and God's daughters as well. They are people who recognize the God of peace as their Father, the Prince of Peace as their leader, and the way of peacemaking as the only Christlike way of life. They look for actions to take that include others and deeds to perform that assert the value of others.

They run the risk of stepping into moments of conflict to do curative peace work, to heal torn relationships, and even do a bit of surgery where needed. And they're also concerned about preventive peacemaking. They look for budding hostilities and help to relieve them while they're still forming and haven't yet reached the explosive stage. They take action in simple, yet powerful ways.

First, they do not judge others by what they've been or what they've done, but by what they are now. The apostle Paul wrote of this insistence on opening the future for others by releasing them from their pasts.

> The very spring of our actions is the love of Christ. . . . This means that our knowledge of men can no longer be based on their outward lives (indeed, even though we knew Christ as a man we do not know him like that any longer). For if a man is in Christ he becomes a new person altogether—the past is finished and gone, everything has become fresh and new. (2 Corinthians 5:14*a*, 16–17)

Second, they look for strengths in others and encourage them. They sense where there are gifts and talents lying dormant or ignored and try to release them. Again, the apostle Paul gets it exactly right from the point of view of the person who is devalued.

> For just as you have many members in one physical body and those members differ in their functions, so we, though many in number, compose one body in Christ and are all members of one another. . . .
> Let us have no imitation Christian love. Let us have a genuine break with evil and a real devotion to good. Let us have real warm affection for one another as between brothers, and a willingness to let the other . . . have the credit. (Romans 12:4–5, 9–10)

To look for opportunities to build up others and encourage them, to help release others to become all they can be in Christ is worth a thousand words of advice.

To share concern for the other's fulfillment, self-discovery, opportunity for service, and meaningful work is better than a thousand criticisms or compliments.

Like their Master, those who follow Jesus act in love, knowing that love is something you do as well as think and feel. They look for opportunities for reconciling, options that include forgiving, and interventions that lead to healing.

Notice: When someone loses control of anger and slaps your face in rage, Jesus calls you to act out forgiveness. Jesus was saying, "Stay vulnerable." Turn an unprotected cheek to say, "I'm not going to back away from you because our relationship matters too much to build walls of defense between us." A second cheek, going a second mile, giving up a second coat, offering a second chance—all these are acts of acceptance. Acts that move us one more step toward reconciliation.

Jesus was a master at simple acts that spoke a million words. To establish a relationship with an outcast minority-group woman, a questionable person in her own society, Jesus simply placed Himself in the position of needing and asking for a favor: "May I have a drink of water from the pitcher you have just drawn from the deep well?" (see John 4:7). But in that act, He set aside social custom, racial prejudice, religious traditions, class distinctions, male-female barriers, and superior-inferior attitudes and fears.

It was a simple act of acceptance, of bridging the two-way need for forgiveness between two nations locked in fear and avoidance of each other. Such unexpected acts of acceptance were His way of life. He invited Himself to dinner with the despised tax collector. He gave caring acceptance in clear acts of love.

He could be surgically sharp when surgery was the loving thing to do. His acts, such as going to the cross, have touched off millions of spoken and written words as people have tried to express the depth of His caring for others. But His acts remain clearer than all the words.

And so it is in our relationships. To forgive, to accept, to move again into right relationship, to be brothers and sisters again are not matters of words. They are deeds, acts, gestures of love, simple steps of acceptance—caring enough to feel the other's pain for a moment and then doing for the other what you would want done for you. It is respecting the other's needs as you respect your own. It is meeting the other on the common ground you share, not demanding that he or she come over to your turf, see things from your point of view, and live or forgive as you prescribe. It is recognizing the other's need to live as an accepted and forgiven person, just as you too need to be accepted and forgiven. It requires mutual acts of love expressed through loving behavior.

Although I've just written a thousand words about loving, accepting, and forgiving acts, one act would say it better. Forgiveness in action is love enacted—embodied—in healing presence.

# 10

# DOES FORGIVING
# INCLUDE
# THE ENEMY?

As a child, the great Russian philosopher and novelist Leo Tolstoy was told by his older brother Nicholas that there was a hidden secret buried in the ancient Zakaz forest in the heart of Russia. *In an unknown spot at the edge of a deep ravine somewhere in the deepest woods a green stick with a secret inscription lies awaiting our discovery. It is no ordinary piece of wood. Carved onto its surface is the ultimate truth in three words—words so powerful that they "would destroy all evil in the hearts of men and bring humanity everything good."*

His brother's story became the central metaphor of Tolstoy's life. He spent his all his years searching for the revelation carved on that green stick. As an old man he wrote, "I still believe today that there is such a truth . . ."[1]

If we were to discover it, the three words would not be unfamiliar. They would be the words each of us has buried away in the darkest corner of our hearts, somewhere by the deep abyss in the floor of our souls. If we found it, it would read *"Love your enemies."*

❧   ❧   ❧

Mirial Buller, a friend in Southern California who grew up in one of the historic peace churches, tells a surprising story. One evening she pulled into her driveway to find a truck parked at the back door of her house and a man loading up the TV and stereo.

"Excuse me, but what are you doing?" she asked him.

"I'm picking up appliances for repairs; the owners called for service," he replied.

Without raising her voice she said, "This is my house; there has been no request. What are you *really* doing here?"

Her kindness, her simple inquiry, her poise disarmed the man. After a long pause, he replied, "I have been without work for months; I have a family to feed. I picked your house at random. I have never done this before. I don't know what to say for myself."

"If you carry the things back inside, I'll wait right here," Mirial replied. "Then I'll give you groceries from my pantry, and I'll move my car from the driveway, and you can go." The man complied, she moved the car, and when he came out, she said, "Just wait. I'll be back with groceries. I will not be calling the police."

Minutes later she reappeared with two large sacks of foodstuff. As she was giving it to the man, two public utility men came up the drive. "So you did call the police," he said. "No, you are free to go," she replied. He backed from the drive and was gone. A few minutes later, he rang the doorbell, and said, "I'm returning the money I took from your dresser drawer. I am deeply sorry."

Months later, a well-dressed man appeared at their door with an envelope. In it was a hundred dollars and a note. "You treated me with a kindness I did not deserve. It was my first attempted theft. It was also my last. I am enclosing a gift for the groceries. I almost messed up my whole life that night, but your response turned me around. I took the food home to my family, then went away to the desert for a spiritual retreat to find my soul once more. I have since found a job and a new sense of direction for my life. Thank you."

My friend Mirial would not recommend her response as a model for anyone else, and she trembles in fear when she remembers that encounter. But she would insist that you follow your intuition in treating another as you would want to be treated—even if you are face-to-face with one who may be your enemy.

⋊  ⋊  ⋊

May Haviland, a member of the Society of Friends—a Quaker—opened the door of her room one night and was astounded to see a burly, dark-haired man rifling her bureau drawers. Quietly she entered the room and closed the door behind her. At the faint click the burglar wheeled, pistol in hand.

"Put that thing down," she said. "I'm going to help you because you must need whatever I have much more than I do, if you have to steal for it."

The burglar, dumbfounded, watched as she opened a secret drawer and pressed her jewelry on him, telling him she was sorry that his need was so urgent. Suddenly the man dropped his gun and fled, taking nothing.

The next day, an unsigned note was in her mailbox. It read: "Madam, I have known only hate and fear. I can deal with them. But I was powerless before your kindness."

Retelling it, May added, "Even guns are silent in the face of love."

⋊  ⋊  ⋊

## What Creates Enemies?

Gandhi once remarked, "I have only three enemies. My favorite enemy, the one most easily influenced for the better, is the British nation. My second enemy, the Indian people, is far more difficult. But my most formidable opponent is a man named Mohandas K. Gandhi. With him I seem to have very little influence."

To come to know our enemies, we must come to know ourselves. Our enemies are not unfamiliar to us. Instead they reflect our inner conflicts, reveal our inner foes, display a great deal about our own shadow side—the dark side of our souls. We participate in the creation of our enemies, not just by accepting their definition of themselves as our opponents or by agreeing with our society's designation of certain persons, groups, or nations as our foes, but by investing them with the fears, denied hates, and hidden revulsions that form our own inner garbage. This garbage reemerges as pictures of the feared other. Pogo, the cartoon character created by Walt Kelly, once said the classic line that has become a legendary truth. "We have met the enemy and they is us."

Forgiving love has a strange power, the power to include the enemy, to refuse to let the enemy define who is what and what is what. Another may define himself or herself as the enemy, but love refuses the definition. Love refuses to relinquish its power to choose how it will behave. It retains the power to confront alienation, not with further alienation, but with acceptance and compassion.

These are strange words in Western culture, where violence has come to be trusted as the last word in resolving difficulties. "Americans not only condone violence, we love it. We love to fight," says Dr. David Abrahamsen, a researcher at Brandeis University who specializes in the study of violence. "Violence by gun is an American trait. We are still living under the legend of the Wild West—where action with a gun was the easiest solution."[2] The proper way to view the enemy was down the barrel of a gun.

Stanford University psychologist Albert Bandura pinpoints why. "The whole culture has changed the violence syndrome into a cool guiltless routine of disposing of problems by disposing of the people who cause the problem."[3] The right way to deal with enmity was to eliminate the enemy.

In a recent year in America, some six thousand persons died of gunshot wounds. Contrast this with Great Britain, where there were fewer than thirty; France, under twenty; Belgium, less than a dozen. "We are a violent people with a violent history," says Arthur Schlesinger Jr., the Pulitzer prize-winning historian and aide to the assassinated President Kennedy. "The instinct for violence has seeped into the bloodstream of our national life."[4] The ever-present threat of the enemy has become a fact of life.

## We Create Violent Myths, Then They Create Us

Behind our penchant for violent actions lies our fascination with violent stories, our addiction to violent films and television programs, and our belief on the necessity of violent resolutions to situations of threat or conflict. Theologian Walter Wink has called the central organizing cluster of beliefs that shape our culture the "myth of redemptive violence."[5]

This myth of conquest of the enemy as a redemptive resolution of evil situations, as a necessary conclusion to scenes of human conflict, as the inevitable and redeeming climax to any drama of injustice, invasion, or injury shapes our view of life and our understanding of how things finally get set right.

But violence is not redemptive. It is cyclical, repetitive, destructive, and self-defeating. Yet the stories our children absorb from cartoons, the dramas we parents watch at night, and the editorials we discuss over breakfast all support the old myth that teaches us to make violence the last word. The final response to the enemy is to become like the enemy. In seeking to rid ourselves of the enemy, we become the enemy. Rather than ridding ourselves of that which we hate, we repeat it, internalize it, become it forever. We have created a myth that makes our eradication of the enemy a virtue to be taught, a goal to be sought.

Our myths become realities since, as we have said, things perceived to be real are real in their consequences; myths believed to be true become the truth of our assumptions. Violence then becomes an integral part of our community life, social fabric, and political structures.

Violence exists in every culture on many levels. There are many forms of hidden violence in the quiet ways a culture forces some social classes or subgroups to be less than human. The violence of prejudice dashes a group's hopes for happiness and shatters its self-respect. The violence of discrimination limits a group's educational, vocational, and social options. The violence of injustice allows some persons to claim entitlement to immediate recourse when abused or defrauded, while other persons are "invisible" and overlooked.

When open violence breaks out, the dominant culture sees its part as "keeping law and order" and the nondominant culture's part as maintaining lawless disorder. This is more difficult to see when one is not a part of the oppressed group unless it is put into words by an inadvertent admission of what is social reality. A spokesman told a rally in Raleigh, North Carolina, "We don't believe in violence, and we don't intend to have any violence if we have to kill every Negro in America." That's what the man said. That's what the culture has often permitted in the dominant culture and exacted from the nondominant subgroups.

Or in response to the self-protective violence of the conservative (to be conservative is to commit oneself to a culture one seeks to conserve), there is the violence advocated by the impatient or disillusioned liberal who, as Robert Fitch puts it, "tremulously anticipates violence before it occurs, celebrates it while it is happening, and justifies it when it is over."[6] When we have put the finishing touches on the myths that explain our violence, they in turn retouch all our other values. And the two extremes—far right and far left— mirror each other. In our enmity we become like those we consider the enemy.

### Where Does It Come From?
### Where Does It Lead?

Some forms of violence in our culture spring from impatience— the impatience of those whose dreams and ideals turn to despair. When affluence, prosperity, and privilege make pleasure-seekers and power-seekers out of a group's upper classes, the lower classes grow impatient waiting for the promised trickle-down.

Other forms of violence arise out of frustration. "Our society is built on success. Success, measured by materialism, creates frustration. Frustration is the wet nurse of violence."

Those who probe deeper say that violence is simply hatred acted out. John Gardner, former secretary of Health, Education, and Welfare, writes, "Hatred triggers violence, violence stirs further hatred, savage responses; hostility begets hostility, and the storm rages on. At some point, the terrifying interplay must have an end."[7]

Violence sometimes is a search for retributive justice—revenge or retaliation when there seems to be no recourse in the courts of the society. If anything "comes natural" from childhood to adulthood, it's the urge to get even. To deliver insult for insult, blow for blow, injury for injury. The law of tit for tat is the oldest law in the world. It is found in the earliest recorded law code, the code of Hammurabi, from ancient Babylon (almost four thousand years old). It is cited in almost all systems of law, including the early biblical records (Exodus 21:23–25; Leviticus 24:19–20; Deuteronomy 19:21).

The classic law of retaliation, *lex talionis* (an eye must be paid with an eye), is usually limited in all civilizations for wrongs done against members of the social order. But the impulse is still second nature when the injury is done by a national enemy, is desired when it is a social enemy, and is sought passionately by many when it is a personal foe. In cultures said to be shaped by Christian values, the last words to penetrate the psyche seem to be those of Jesus in His central teaching, the Sermon on the Mount. "You've always heard it said: An eye for an eye, and a tooth for a tooth; but I tell you, don't resist evil; but if anyone strikes you on the right cheek, turn the other to him also" (Matthew 5:38–39, paraphrased from the KJV).

The quotable one-time premier of Russia, Nikita Krushchev, once said in a press conference with American news reporters: "We Communists have many things in common with the teachings of Jesus Christ. My sole difference with Christ is that when someone hits me on the right cheek, I hit him on the left so hard that his head falls off."[8] His point of view was not foreign to that of most of the newsmen or the editors who so gladly reported it.

## What If We Took Jesus Seriously?

Of all the "hard sayings" of Jesus, none seems so difficult, so counterintuitive, as His statement about turning the other cheek. It is not that those who understand what He meant by it and why He taught this nonviolent response have rejected it and turned away from faith because of the impracticality of the demand. Instead His teaching is constantly softened, spiritualized, and relegated to another time period or gently dismissed as something to be affirmed as an ideal in a utopian world but not to be seriously followed in the real world. It is a difficult teaching, a jolting demand. It challenges a most basic human right—the right of self-defense.

"Self-defense has become not only a right, but a duty," an American writer wrote recently. That's a proper opinion to most men, who speak of "the manly art of self-defense" as if it were an unalienable right of humanity, or to women who trust the protection of a "Saturday night special" as essential. When violence is seen as the necessary safeguard for personal security, we all lose. To equate violence with personal strength is to believe an illusion. It requires far greater strength to practice nonviolence than to let anger follow the natural course of coercion or explosive retaliation.

In personal conflicts, it's usually the one in the wrong who clenches a fist first. It's the one who is beaten mentally and morally who tries to settle the conflict with muscle or maneuvering. When a person is wrong and knows it, the temper is bound to flare, fists to clench, knuckles to whiten. Violence is usually an unconscious confession of weakness, inferiority, and cowardice in facing up to the true state of things. In the long view, violence is, has been, and always will be the loser's way.

Violence never resolves violence. Hate cannot overcome hate. Evil is never destroyed by evil. It may be temporarily arrested or postponed, but payday comes. Revenge is always self-defeating. The only antidote to hate is love; only goodness can extinguish the fires of evil. If you let the enemy's evil actions determine your reactions, or let another's violence move you to violence, you lose the opportunity to help and heal that comes only through love.

## Finding the Way of Enemy Love

"All they that take the sword shall perish [by] the sword," said Jesus Christ (Matthew 26:52 KJV). In contrast to our human way of violence, Christ called us to unclench our fists and learn the power of love. "But I tell you, Do not resist an evil person. . . . Love your enemies and pray for those who persecute you, that you may be sons of your Father in heaven" (Matthew 5:39, 44–45 NIV).

His disciples apparently took Him at His word. It is rarely reported, but true, that for the first two hundred years of Christianity, not only nonviolence, but nonresistance was the practice of Christians. In following this approach the church not only survived, but grew in numbers and strength through three centuries of nonresistance to vicious persecution. Enemy-love was the measure of authentic Christian love.

Those Christians who seek to follow—to imitate—Christ in life refuse violence because, as Jesus taught, love alone can conquer hatred; only love can defeat violence, and the way of God is not in our seizing power and claiming to be on the side of justice. The only place in the New Testament where we are commanded to imitate Christ is in replicating his model of nonviolent, nonresistant love. God and justice will triumph in the end. No evil means can assist. That was Christ's conviction. And in the crucial argument on nonviolence, the apostle Peter (a reported violent man) wrote: "When he suffered, he made no threats. [When he was abused, he did not respond with violence.]  Instead, he entrusted himself to him who judges justly, . . . leaving us an example that we should follow in his steps" (see 1 Peter 2:21, 23 NIV).

This total faith in God's eternal future lets those who make

Christ's way their own accept suffering without violence and revenge. This was the way of Christ. Is it not to be our way, too?

We who love retaliation and revenge can be thankful that God does not! When God walked among us in Jesus Christ, He lived—and called us to live—in a far different way. He chose to show patience, even at the cost of suffering. He chose to forgive, even at the cost of His life.

## What If It Is Painful, Insulting, Hard?

So the person who follows Christ in living by love responds in a new way to the person who abuses. Sure, he cares when someone slaps his face, but he cares more about the other person than about the insult. By turning the other cheek he is saying, "What I care about is you, friend. I don't want you to go on in bitter, harsh anger. I may have the human right to strike back, but I pass it by because I feel a responsibility for you before God. I take the humiliating, defenseless way, but not out of cowardice. Obviously, it demands more bravery and more strength of character to control anger than to obey it. But I refuse to retaliate because you are far more important. Your discovery of the love and forgiveness of God is of greater value than my getting even." In small insults that matter little, this advice is possible and practical. But in the harsh, painful conflicts when you feel the full weight of the other's contempt, it seems almost impossible.

But when Christ spoke of turning the other cheek he was speaking, not of daily irritations, but of the lowest expression of contempt. "If someone strikes you on the right cheek," He said. What did that mean? If you are right-handed, you would naturally strike another on the left cheek (Matthew 5:39 NIV). To strike on the right would demand an awkward contortion—unless you struck disdainfully with the back of the hand. In Christ's time, as in ours, to slap another with the back of your hand was a doubly insulting arrogant flick of hate. Thus Christ was saying, "To even the lowest of insults, turn the other cheek; accept the insult without resentment."

When slapped inhumanely, he accepted it unflinchingly, turning the other cheek even as He asked, "If I said something wrong, . . . testify as to what is wrong. But if I spoke the truth, why did you strike me?" (John 18:23 NIV). Peter, who stood by watching, later wrote: "When he was insulted he offered no insult in return" (1 Peter 2:23).

To this Paul added: "Never take vengeance into your own hands, my dear friends: stand back and let God punish if he will. For it is written: Vengeance belongeth unto me: I will recompense" (Romans 12:19).

> And these are God's words:
>     If thine enemy hunger, feed him;
>     If he thirst, give him to drink:
>     For in so doing [you speak not to his rage but to his conscience].
>
> Don't allow yourself to be overpowered by evil. Take the offensive—
> overpower evil with good! (Romans 12:20–21)

That is the strategy of the utterly unexpected. A Canadian friend once wrote me: "I once slapped another in the face during a conflict we had. He got me mad. I had anger in me, and I slapped him. When I did, he silently looked at me, then he turned the other cheek. I was stunned."

"But," you ask, "if I turn the other cheek, how do I know it will work?" There is no guarantee of effectiveness. It may not result in moving you toward reconciliation. After all, love is not a strategy. It is a way of life—the life of love modeled by Jesus. One does not follow it because it is more secure, but because it is moral, principled, and faithful to the values believed to be eternal.

Obviously, it's a difficult way. Any appeal to the enemy's conscience bears great risk. But so do all the valuable things in life. The choice to love is the most risky choice in the universe. But in the end, it is the only alternative that will endure. Of all our motivations and decisions, only love endures.

In a world of violence, the alternative that offers hope of changing the violent course of human history is not more violence, or more invincible violence, but the way of peacemaking, of nonviolent, nonresistant love.

Thus, we may conclude that all Christians are peacemakers, indeed, pacifists, since all believe that the Cross, not the sword, is God's last word; that love and forgiveness, not coercion and violence, are the heart of the gospel. The difference among Christians is not over this central issue, but over how much provocation is necessary, how much justification is required before one departs the way of Jesus and re-

sorts to the way of violence. There are followers of Jesus who are willing to suffer very little threat before they become pragmatic and justify the use of violence to insure safety on their own terms. In contrast,
some followers believe that the way of Jesus can be embraced without resorting to the use of force at any point.

Jesus' words are unmistakable; the voice of the New Testament is
clear; the practice of the early church is consistent—nonviolent love
is the Jesus way. The choice is present in every age: Shall one follow
the way of Christ in loving the enemy, or shall one join the dominant
culture and justify violent alternatives?

Will retaliation be our last word? Or will reconciling love and
courage be used only when it seems advisable, or appears defensi-
ble, or seems practical? Or will it be forgiveness, as it was for our Lord?

## What If It Means Your Life?

In the 1919 massacre of Armenian peoples by the neighboring
Turks, over a million people were summarily murdered. Many stories
of intense suffering and tragedy are all that remain as memories, but
among them stand those accounts of unbelievable courage, such as
the one that follows.

≻    ≻    ≻

A military unit attacked a village of Armenian Christians, killing
all adults, all males, and all small children, taking only the young
women as hostages. An officer, raiding a home, shot the parents, gave
the daughters to his soldiers, but kept the beautiful oldest daughter
for himself. For months, until he found another who pleased him
more, she was forced into servitude and sexual abuse. At last, pushed
out of his house, she escaped from the military camp and slowly rebuilt her life, ultimately completing training as a nurse.

One night, while on duty in a Turkish hospital, she was caring
for a desperately ill patient in intensive care, and she recognized the
face behind the bandages and tubes—it was her former captor and
abuser, the murderer of her parents. He was comatose, and without
constant care he would not survive. A long and difficult convalescence
followed, with the patient too ill to be aware of his surroundings or
of those giving him care. One day, as he was awaking to the reality

around him, the Turkish doctor said to him, "You are a very fortunate man. Had it not been for the devoted care of this nurse who watched over you in your brush with death, you would never have made it. You would be a dead man."

The officer looked long at the nurse. "I've wanted for the last three days to ask you—we have met before, have we not?"

"Yes," she replied, "we have met before."

"Why didn't you just let me die when you had the opportunity? You would have had every chance, every right to kill me, would you not?"

"No," she said, "I would not, because I am a follower of Him who said, 'Love your enemies.'"[9]

## Notes

1. Adapted from Henri Troyat, *Tolstoy*, trans. Nancy Amphoux (Garden City, N.Y.: Doubleday, 1967), 6.
2. David Abrahamsen, in "Hostility," *Daily News Record*, Harrisonburg, Va., 12 June 1968.
3. Ibid.
4. Ibid.
5. Walter Wink, *Engaging the Powers* (Minneapolis: Fortress, 1992).
6. Robert Fitch, "Is America Really Sick?" *U.S. News & World Report*, 10 June 1968, 47.
7. John Gardner, in "Hostility," *Daily News Record*, Harrisonburg, Va., 12 June 1968.
8. Nikita Khrushchev, as cited by Stewart Meachem in address given to Intercollegiate Peace Fellowship, Bluffton College, Bluffton, Ohio, 31 March 1960.
9. Adapted from Geoffrey Wainright, *Doxology: The Praise of God in Worship, Doctrine, and Life* (New York: Oxford Univ. Press, 1980), 434.

# DOES FORGIVING LEAD TO AGAPE LOVE?

I arrived in the city of Everywhere early one morning. It was cold, and there were flurries of snow on the ground. As I stepped from the train to the platform I noticed that the baggage man and the redcap were warmly attired in heavy coats and gloves, but oddly enough, they wore no shoes. Repressing my impulse to ask the reason for this odd practice, I went into the station and inquired the way to the hotel. My curiosity, however, was increased by the discovery that no one in the station wore any shoes. Boarding the streetcar, I saw that my fellow travelers were likewise barefoot; and upon arriving at the hotel I found that the bellhop, the clerk, and the residents were all devoid of shoes.

Unable to restrain myself longer, I asked the manager what the practice meant.

"What practice?" said he.

"Why," said I, pointing to his bare feet, "why don't you wear shoes in this town?"

"Ah," said he, "that is just it. Why don't we?"

"But what is the matter? Don't you believe in shoes?"

"Believe in shoes, my friend! I should say we do. That is the first article of our creed, shoes. They are indispensable to the well-being of humanity. Such frostbite, cuts, sores, and suffering as shoes prevent! It is wonderful!"

"Well, then, why don't you wear them?" I asked, bewildered.

"Ah," he said thoughtfully, "that is just it. Why don't we?"

Though considerably nonplussed, I checked in, secured my room, and went directly to the coffee shop. There I deliberately sat down by an amiable-looking but barefoot gentleman. Friendly enough, he suggested, after we had eaten, that we look about the city.

The first thing we noticed upon emerging from the hotel was a huge brick structure of impressive proportions. He pointed to this with pride.

"You see that?" said he. "That is one of our outstanding shoe manufacturing establishments!"

"A *what?*" I asked in amazement. "You mean you make shoes there?"

"Well, not exactly," said he, a bit abashed. "We talk there about the art and science of making shoes, and, believe me, we have one of the most brilliant young fellows you have ever heard. He talks most thrillingly and convincingly every week on this great subject of shoes. Just yesterday he moved the people profoundly with his exposition of the necessity of shoe wearing. Many broke down and wept. It was really wonderful!"

"But why don't they wear them?" said I insistently.

"Ah, that is just it. Why don't we?"

Just then, as we turned down a side street, I saw through a cellar window a cobbler actually making a pair of shoes. Excusing myself from my friend, I burst into the little shop and asked the shoemaker how it happened that his shop was not overrun with customers. "Nobody wants my shoes," he said. "They just talk about them."

"Give me what pairs you have ready," I said eagerly, and paid him thrice the amount he modestly asked. Hurriedly, I returned to my friend and offered them to him, saying, "Here, my friend, one of these pairs will surely fit you. Take them; put them on. They will save untold suffering."

"Ah, thank you," he said, with embarrassment, "but you don't understand. It just isn't being done. The front families, well, that is just it. Why don't we?"

And coming out of the city of Everywhere, over and over and

over that question rang in my ears: "Why don't we? Why don't we? Why don't we?"

➤    ➤    ➤

The parable of the barefoot Christians was written more than a hundred years ago by an English clergyman, Hugh Price Hughes. The city he calls Everywhere could be Boston, Houston, Toronto, or Toledo —as well as London or Dublin. It is anywhere. It is everywhere. It is where people know the most basic, obvious steps toward right relationships but do not take them. The shoes on their feet are to be the good news of peace (Ephesians 6:15), yet they go barefoot.

The most basic footwear of healthful human relations is the rule of mutual love, often called "the law of reciprocity" or "the Golden Rule." "Act toward your neighbor as you would want your neighbor to act toward you."

Mature love is mutual love, reciprocal love, love that sees the other with equal regard, love that prizes the other as one values the self.

The goal of *adult maturation* is to achieve mutuality, that state in which the other's needs become considered alongside one's own.

The goal of *adult love* is to arrive at a point, as Harry Stack Sullivan used to say, where another's safety and security are as important as one's own.

The goal of *Christian spirituality* is to come to the place where our neighbor's needs and welfare are as high a concern as our own wants and wishes.

All these are contained in the words we call the Golden Rule. It is the best-known, most frequently quoted statement of the greatest figure in history—Jesus Christ. When first given nineteen centuries ago, it came as a summarization of the entire Jewish law on "how to live with humans." It is still unsurpassed as a basic rule of human relations and worthy of the wisest thinker's consideration. The idea of a fair basis of concern and respect for others is an old one, a multicultural one that emerges in many religious traditions and in many cultural worldviews.

Confucius said, "What you do not want done to yourself, do not do to others." Zoroaster, the ancient Persian, taught that "nature alone is good which refrains from doing unto another whatsoever is not good for itself." Hinduism: "This is the sum of duty: Do naught unto others that would cause you pain if done to you." Buddhism: "Hurt not others in ways that you yourself would find hurtful." Judaism: "What is hateful to yourself, do to no other. That is the entire law; all the rest is commentary."

The Greek philosophers each had a unique way of phrasing it, such as Epictetus: "What thou avoidest suffering thyself seek not to impose on others." Socrates: "Do not do to others what would anger you if done to you by others."

Jesus gave the law of reciprocity a different perspective. Rather than offering it as a prohibition, He gave it as a commission.

"Treat other people exactly as you would like to be treated by them—this is the essence of all true religion" (Matthew 7:12).

The newness, the uniqueness of Christ's rule of life lies in the commission to act lovingly; to do the thoughtful, considerate, sympathetic thing; to risk acting in love when there is no guarantee, perhaps no likelihood of its being reciprocated. It is not unique just because it is a positive action. Even beneficial actions can rise from evil motives. Positive actions can be positively wrong.

For example, the Golden Rule of capitalism is frequently cited in a positive form, but it can be given a positive spin that not only spins, but is twisted. For example, the Golden Rule of business is not just to do business in a way that is good business for both the buyer and the seller. (Who can question it when "business is business"?) But the law of mutuality Jesus taught requires that one do business in a way that honors the other's needs as you would want your own needs honored—not just that the profits go both ways.

The Golden Rule can be copied, contorted, caricatured in many ways: "Do unto others before they do it to you." Or, "Do unto others what you accuse them of doing unto you." Or, "Do unto others what they have just done to you." Just because it is two-way does not mean it is the right way. For those who believe, "My way is Yahweh," there is no righteousness, justice, or possible equality.

In warfare the rule is positive yet destructive. "In war," says Dr. MacIver, professor of political science at Columbia University, "the principle must be do to the enemy as he would do to you, but do it first."[1] That's merely the savage law of retaliation. "Do back to others as they have done to you." Or even worse, "Do to others as you expect them to do to you."

What a vast difference between the human reaction of doing as we *are* done by and Christ's call to do as we would *wish* to be done by. Christ's standard—do the same as you wish from others—provides an unselfish rule of thumb for gauging your actions and attitudes toward others.

The Golden Rule is balanced to protect both sides against the selfishness that always lurks beneath the surface of human beings. There are moral philosophers who point out that the rule should read, "Do unto others as they would have you do unto them."

They insist that Christ's wording, "Do as you would have them do unto you," is self-centered, drawing the lines by what you want instead of what your neighbor wants. But to always do what your neighbor wants or asks would not be love. It would be neutrality, disinterest, or indifference to the other's good. It would be a servile slavery to another's wishes. A doctor would give heroin to an addict because he wants it; a girl would surrender sex to a boy because he asks it. That is not love, as any parent knows. Love is a concern for your neighbor. So if you love, give and do for another as you wish to be treated.

The benchmark for your action—do what you wish from others —comes out again and again in Christ's teaching. In fact, the Golden Rule is simply the practical application of the second greatest of all commandments: "To love your neighbor as yourself."

You are to love the other as yourself because the other *is* as yourself. He is like you; she is similar to you. There is only one and the same basis for prizing the self or valuing the other. The Bible gives that command over a dozen times. Your self-respect should be so high that not for the world—or for anything in it—will you stoop to demean your character or do a deed unworthy of yourself. Hold yourself in high regard, Christ taught, but no higher than you hold your neighbor, in no different way than you uphold your neighbor. He is like, she is not unlike, you.

In the biblical vision, love for self and love for neighbor are not two loves, but one and the same love with two different aspects. The same basis by which I know myself to be precious is equally true for you. To love oneself rightly is to love the other equally.

Christ applied this rule to the most crucial areas of life. In love: Love your neighbor as you love yourself (Matthew 22:39). In *forgiveness:* Forgive the other as you wish to be forgiven (Matthew 6:14–15). In *service:* Do unto others as you would have them do unto you (Matthew 7:12).

Putting this law of reciprocity into personal relationships means at least the following.

- We listen to others as we want to be listened to.
- We offer help to others where we would expect help.
- We seek to understand others' viewpoints as we would be understood.
- We care more about dealing fairly with our neighbor than we worry about being cheated by our neighbor.
- We offer praise and appreciation to others as we would want to be appreciated.
- We treat employees, creditors, and debtors as we would wish to be treated by those in authority over us.
- We pass on no gossip about another that we would not want circulated about ourselves.
- We give others the benefit of the doubt in questionable circumstances, as we would do for ourselves.
- We discard all prejudices that we would resent as unfair if we were members of the race or group suffering discrimination.
- We respect, defend, and accept a person of any race, culture, or class as we would wish to be regarded by them. We will love our neighbor as we love ourselves, and in so doing put into practice Christ's second greatest commandment.

Christ rooted the commandment of reciprocity in what He called the first and greatest commandment. "Thou shalt love the Lord thy God with all thy heart, and with all thy soul, and with all thy mind" (Matthew 22:37 KJV).

## Going the Extra Distance: "The Second Mile"

Jesus used a revealing metaphor—going the second mile. In the culture of the day, a Palestinian citizen could be pressed into service as a carrier for one mile. Members of the occupying Roman army, civil servants, or postal couriers could demand such service at any time.

Jesus suggested the totally unexpected response. When asked to bear a load for one mile as your civil obligation, volunteer for a second.

The visual image this aroused in His hearers borders on comedy. Imagine the Roman soldier reaching for his pack, and the Jewish bearer gladly refusing to give up the heavy load. "No, no; that was only a mile downhill. Let me carry it up the next one."

Difficult as this may have seemed to oppressed citizens of an abused nation, Jesus' teaching offered a way to claim one's freedom, to move beyond being powerless to actually defining one's own life and service. Yet His teaching is still a difficult option. The second mile is among the most painful journeys we will make.

Once when mediating a dispute between two mature men—a disagreement that had begun in their profession but had seeped through into community, family, and church life—I first learned how long the second mile appeared to each.

When I talked with the first party, he said, "I've bent over backward to settle this thing. I've gone the second and now the third mile, but he won't come an inch to meet me."

But the other man said, "I've already gone the second mile, and I'm not going an inch farther."

One had come two miles, the other three, and they were still miles apart. They were not even within shouting distance—at least neither could hear the other.

Isn't the first mile the distance from blind self-defensiveness to sympathetic understanding of the other? To come that first mile is nothing extra. It's only minimum humanity. No two persons are ever more than "two miles" apart. If they will each accept the obvious responsibility of one to another, they can and will meet. As brothers, each owes the other a listening ear, one might assume, a willingness to hear what the other is actually saying, and an understanding mind to see the other's point of view.

"To walk the second mile"—this fascinating metaphor from Jesus Christ—may have risen from His own experience. As a young man, Christ may have been asked to carry a pack for the thousand paces specified as a Roman mile and, if no relief came in sight, may have been forced to carry it until another hapless citizen appeared. Obviously this law was less than popular. But Jesus had the gall to say, "If anybody forces you to go a mile with him, do more—go two miles with him" (Matthew 5:41). What's worse, He also said, "If a man wants to sue you for your shirt, let him have your coat as well. . . . If someone slaps you on the right cheek, turn and offer him your left" (Matthew 5:39–40 NEB).

To sum up His teaching in simple words: *Always live above the law.* Do more than just "doing your duty." Aim higher than minimum living. Live your forgiveness as a way of life—constantly and consistently. To live forgiveness is to give wholehearted acceptance to others. There is no forgiveness without genuine acceptance of the other person as he or she is.

"Open your hearts to one another as Christ has opened his heart to you," Paul wrote to the Romans (Romans 15:7). To do this is to accept another in a way that takes real responsibility for him. It is an accepting love that gets its sleeves rolled up and its hands dirty in helping, serving, lifting, and changing others' lives into the full freedom of forgiveness—God's forgiveness and ours.

Forgiveness is not leaving a person with the burden of "something to live down." It is offering the other someone to live "with."

Recently the head of a large corporation told me, "Yesterday, the president of one of the East's larger electric utility companies spent a whole morning negotiating a simple contract with me! 'We know your principles,' he said to me, 'and we're worried that the contract might not be fair enough to you. Do you mind if we go over it once more to make sure your side is equally fair?'"

"Second-mile religion" is a matter of love. The first mile offers love to your friendly neighbor. The second mile offers to love your enemy, adversary, or competitor. And it is a decision you make. To love is to will and desire your neighbor's good, whether you like him or not. The Good Samaritan may not have liked the poor, beaten man in the ditch. But he acted in his behalf. He did something about the man's tragedy.

"This," said Jesus, "is love." Such love is not dependent at all on the nature, beauty, or niceness of the one loved. It depends completely on the one doing the loving. Love can be—and will be—emotional, because there are natural affections that rise in our hearts. But, far more, Christian love (agape) is volitional. It's a decision to seek the other's good.

Jesus does not command that we like our enemies with warm affection; we cannot always command our emotions. But we can command our actions. We can act lovingly toward others, whether we like them or not.

## Agape as Benevolence, Obedience, Sacrifice, or More?

This contradiction between feeling and choice, between emotion and volition, between liking and loving has been resolved in four different ways by Christians throughout the centuries.

The first is by defining Christian agape love as *benevolence*. It is shown in loving the unlovely and the unlovable in generous self-giving. This views *love* as a willing generosity and *forgiveness* as an undeserved gift. The second-mile behavior is based on the goodness of the lover. Yet this view belittles the beloved even in the act of loving. It is less than worthy of what Christ both taught and demonstrated.

The second solution is to define agape love as *willing obedience*. It loves the other out of obedient altruism and the duty and obligation to the commandment to love. This gives love a consistent vigor and stability, but it evokes resistance in the one loving and resentment in the one loved. No one feels affirmed by love given out of duty. Forgiveness, in this perspective, is an obligation owed if one is also to be forgiven.

The third solution is to *love sacrificially*. Agape love is seen as willing self-sacrifice. In giving oneself, one expresses an unconditional love that accepts the other regardless of the cost. But self-sacrifice may be ultimately motivated by self-centeredness. "See how I ask nothing for myself; you always come first" is finally a statement of pride. Forgiveness, in this perspective, is substitutional, vicarious. The forgiver bears the pain of the other's act and his or her own anger and lets the other go free. This vertical forgiveness may be necessary in alienated acts of injury where no relationship has ever or will ever exist, but in ongoing relationships it is destructive.

The fourth solution is to *love in equal regard*. At this level of love, we prize others as having equal worth, as being loved by God to the extent they were worth the cost of Calvary, as being made worthy by the presence of God within and among us. The teaching that we love our neighbors as ourselves stretches from the Pentateuch to the Epistles. Equal regard values each person as an end in himself, as an irreducibly valuable being intrinsically. Forgiveness, seen in this light, is mutual, reciprocal, and two-way. It is reconciliation between persons who stand equally before God, whether they recognize it yet or not.

*Agape,* when seen as equal regard, can include all the previous definitions. It is benevolent—generous and inclusive—but it seeks to work itself out of this superior position as rapidly as possible. It is

obedient, but not for the sake of obedience itself. It is self-sacrifi-
cial, but not out of righteous superiority. The motivation for self-
sacrifice springs from a recognition of the worth of all persons. In
taking this worth as ultimately important, it refuses to participate in
the violation of self or other. It sacrifices self in the interest of love
emphasized by equal regard for all humankind.

⤐    ⤐    ⤐

Once upon a time, two brothers shared a threshing floor where
they threshed the village's grain and shared the portion which fell
to them as payment for their services. . .

So begins one of the oldest stories of mutuality from the Middle East. It occurs in Urdu, Sanskrit, and in Biblical Hebrew in the
Midrash—commentaries on the Hebrew Scriptures—as a story of
reciprocal caring. The rabbinic heritage used it to explain why Mount
Moriah was chosen as the location for the temple. It was on this lime-
stone anticline that the threshing floor stood.

. . . Each evening the brothers divided the grain received as payment into two equal parts and carried their sacks home to pour in
their granaries. The elder brother stored his grain, then went in to
dinner with his wife and their twelve children. The younger brother emptied his sack and went in to dine alone, for he had no wife or
children. Later that night, he would lie sleepless in bed. "My brother insists that I take half the grain each day," he said to himself. "It is
not fair. He has fourteen mouths to feed and I have but one. He insists that I take half, but I must increase his share." So he would rise
from his bed in the darkness, scoop out a great sack of grain, carry it
across the threshing floor and stealthily pour it in his brother's granary.

In the early morning the older brother would awake and lie ru-
minating. "When I grow old, I will have twelve children to care for
me, but my brother has none. He insists that I take half the grain,
but it is not fair. He must lay up for the future. How can I right this
injustice?" And he would rise in the darkness, scoop out a great sack
of grain, carry it across the threshing floor, and secretively pour it in
his brother's granary.

One night—perhaps there was an eclipse—the brothers' timing
was wrong. In the darkness, they met in the middle of the threshing

floor, recognized each other's voices, dropped their sacks to the ground, and fell into each other's arms.

And God said, "That is where My temple will stand—where two brothers care for each other's needs with equal concern as for their own."

This is the equal regard called *agape*. Where such love is, God is.

### Note

1. Ernest Trice Thompson, *Sermon on the Mount* (Richmond: Knox, 1946), 117–18.

# STUDY GUIDE

When we pray the Lord's Prayer we ask for God to forgive us our debts as we forgive the debts of others. This puts us in a difficult position and, indeed, Christianity is often rejected by some because of Christ's injunction to love your enemies. When we do forgive, at times there is not much change. There is little action, and though we say we forgive, our hearts have remnants of hurt, anger, and rejection.

This study guide will help you to move from assimilation and basic understanding of the text to implementation of the principles herein. Do not become discouraged, because forgiveness is a difficult process and only fully accomplished by God's sovereign grace. These restatements of the text, questions for application, and Scriptures for meditation are meant to reinforce this message and help move it from your head to your heart, hands, and feet. God bless you on the path to forgiveness.

# Chapter One

POINTS FOR CONSIDERATION

1. It is natural for us to feel that an offender should pay for wrong-doing, whereas forgiveness seems like an easy way out.

2. Though equal payment, or restitution, seems fair, it turns out that offenses can't practically be paid for, nor do we have the power or position to do this adequately.

3. Revenge simply brings us to the sinful level of our enemy and can cause counterattacks by the other person, which escalates the conflict.

4. Resentment and bitterness seem to be self-protective but actually paralyze us and keep us in bondage, adding to the hurt inflicted upon us.

5. Forgiveness can bring true reconciliation, healing, and the renewed ability to love both God and our neighbor.


REFLECT AND ACT

1. Which of these responses—(1) demand equal repayment; (2) require some restitution; (3) seek revenge; (4) brood in resentment; (5) all of the above; or (6) none of the above—occurs to you naturally during the first shock of injury?

2. Is it a great temptation to go into denial rather than face the injury done to you? (Denial is pretending superiority; putting the injury behind you quickly; refusing to think about the injury, or talk about it, or work it through.)


SCRIPTURE MEDITATION
*Matthew 6:14–15*

## Chapter Two

POINTS FOR CONSIDERATION

1. Much teaching on forgiveness centers on the benefits to the forgiver, rather than healing the relationship with the person who needs to be forgiven.

2. Forgiveness is not just a change of attitude but an active process of restoring a relationship through repentance.

3. The cross of Christ is the ultimate model of the cost of forgiveness and the difficulties we may face if we choose to work at reconciliation.

4. In forgiving we accept others as Christ accepted us—both the hurt and the person who caused it.

5. The Cross is the greatest example of forgiveness because Christ prayed for God's forgiveness of enemies, executioners, and uncaring onlookers in the midst of a painful death.

REFLECT AND ACT

1. When you find forgiveness difficult, you are helped by remembering Christ's prayer on the cross: "Father, forgive them, for they know not what they do."

2. When has a mere change of attitude not been enough to effect complete forgiveness toward someone else? Why?

SCRIPTURE MEDITATION
*Matthew 18:15*

# Chapter Three

POINTS FOR CONSIDERATION

1. One of the reasons it is so difficult to forgive is because it is so hard to understand what lies behind another's hurtful words or acts.

2. When we forgive we need to have "double vision," seeing the behavior as unacceptable yet seeing the other person as precious in spite of the wrongdoing.

3. Understanding, valuing, and loving the other person are all prerequisites to forgiveness. Restoring an attitude of love is the first step toward reconciliation.

4. Every person, no matter how terrible his deeds, still has worth and is loved by God. Wrongdoing does not destroy a person's value.

5. While we were God's enemies, God came in Jesus to reconcile us to each other and to God's own Self. Since God took the initiative toward us, should we not take the initiative with those who wrong us?

REFLECT AND ACT

1. The author asks, "How can you forgive?" What is his answer when you are faced with a huge cost, serious pain, or intense anger?

2. When have you failed to forgive because it seemed impossible to understand what really happened or where the person was coming from? What have you learned about empathy with persons you dislike or with whom you disagree?

SCRIPTURE MEDITATION
*1 John 4:20*

# Chapter Four

POINTS FOR CONSIDERATION

1. Forgiveness does not necessarily get easier the second time around but remains a difficult process with many steps, each of which requires an act of will.

2. True and complete, rather than superficial forgiveness is rare because it demands so much of us, but the freedom and healing are worth the price.

3. Some of us may not be aware that what we consider forgiveness is really only memory fatigue, tolerance, or indifference.

4. Restored relationships are rarely what they were before conflict. They can either become more intimate because of the positive results of a sensitive encounter or more remote to avoid similar occurrences.

5. Forgiveness is not a one-time thing that ends all conflict but a process that continues to bring healing over time.

REFLECT AND ACT

1. Can you recall a time when, instead of working at genuine forgiveness, you chose to be tolerant of the other, to overlook the injury, to avoid facing the pain? Could you look again at the unhealed scars?

2. Have you ever gone through the forgiveness process and arrived at a deeper and more satisfying relationship than before? What did you learn that you will remember the next time?

SCRIPTURE MEDITATION
*Genesis 50:15–21*

# Chapter Five

POINTS FOR CONSIDERATION

1. Anger is one of our least-understood emotions, yet the one we should know most about because of the damage it can do to others and the injury it can do to our own souls.

2. Anger can be helpful or harmful depending upon the reasons, how we handle it, and the outcome for ourselves and for others. Negative anger creates walls and distance; positive anger seeks to break down walls and reduce distance.

3. A temper is a sign of weak impulse controls, although repressed anger is also unhealthy. Anger that is channeled positively and expressed constructively can achieve positive results.

4. You need to be able to deal effectively with your own anger as well as allowing others to work through theirs in order to move toward reconciliation.

5. Anger can move very quickly from something like irritability to rage, so we need to have checkpoints to stop it.

REFLECT AND ACT

1. Review the chapter and assess how your anger can become imbalanced. How can you improve and discipline your anger to work positively in the forgiveness process?

2. Do you have a problem with allowing others to express their own anger? In what ways do you react that may not allow the other person to successfully process their anger?

SCRIPTURE MEDITATION
*Ephesians 4:25–32*

# Chapter Six

1. In order to achieve good results, confession needs boundaries: to the right person, at the right level of detail, with the right purposes.

2. True guilt is a God-given gift that lets us see and experience the nature of our sin; when confessed, it becomes an important part of the redemptive process.

3. Repentance actually has four stages, none of which can be ignored: facing your sin, confessing to the appropriate party, determining not to repeat it, and living in the freedom of release.

4. Confession includes the admission of complete dependence on the grace and strength of Jesus Christ through His atoning sacrifice.

5. True surrender to God means the giving up of our self-life apart from Christ, rather than simply denying ourselves everything we enjoy.

Reflect and Act

1. Review the steps to both confession and repentance above. Which ones do you tend to downplay or ignore and why?

2. Are you a person with too much guilt, not enough guilt, or an appropriate amount? How has this affected your overall dealing with sin?

Scripture Meditation
*Psalm 51:3–4*

## Chapter Seven

Points for Consideration

1. In marriage there must be a mutual willingness for acceptance and growth, rather than using forgiveness as subtle condemnation.

2. We need to give our spouse the freedom to be an individual, respecting his strengths, accepting his weaknesses, and allowing him the right to his own thoughts, feelings, and actions.

3. Active, sincere listening is the most important part of genuine communication and invites each other to grow, especially in the forgiveness process.

4. Faithfulness goes beyond sexual fidelity and includes the willingness to work through differences, to solve conflicts, and to meet the other partner's deepest needs, which sometimes requires forgiving love.

5. Love sets the other person free to be human—that is, to express herself (or himself), including his (or her) faults, without condemnation.

Reflect and Act

1. In what areas do you tend to want your spouse to measure up to your desires and expectations rather than allowing your spouse the freedom to choose? How can you change this?

2. How have you gotten into conflict and misunderstanding with your spouse because you weren't really listening to his (or her) intentions, needs, or desires?

Scripture Meditation
*1 Corinthians 13:4–7*

# Chapter Eight

1. Prejudice is learned opinion, and it can be unlearned. We rarely change such deeply held values except in new relationships that expose old biases.

2. Jesus Christ showed no trace of prejudice in a very bigoted world, yet by the life He lived became a victim of it in His death.

3. Criticism and prejudice go hand in hand and backbiting usually exalts the two parties at the expense of the person being discussed.

4. When we need to judge or criticize we need to do so fairly, lovingly, and humbly—attempting to lift up others rather than condemn them.

5. We can never completely know all the facts or the entire person, so we should make partial, not total, judgments of others.


REFLECT AND ACT
1. When it comes to judging or forgiving the actions of others, are you aware when your responses are tinted by your prejudices? Identify those whom you tend to favor or disfavor.

2. When has seemingly legitimate concern for others actually turned into criticism behind the back, or gossip? How can this be avoided?


SCRIPTURE MEDITATION
*Matthew 7:1–5*

# Chapter Nine

POINTS FOR CONSIDERATION

1. Forgiveness, when it results in mutual two-way change, opens the door to reciprocal and humble outreach on the part of both the forgiver and the one being forgiven.

2. One of the major ministries of the church is picking up the pieces of broken lives and seeking to bring about individual wholeness, relational depth, and corporate unity.

3. Our tendency when others need help is to offer advice, evaluation, or criticism, when presence, concern, service, and just plain encouragement usually work better.

4. Restoring relationships can never be a matter of simple apology or sincere intentions but getting on the other's turf and loving him (or her) in deeds as well as words.

5. Just as Jesus did, we need to perform "unexpected acts of acceptance" that overcome initial barriers between people.

REFLECT AND ACT

1. Have you reached out and helped someone in your local congregation whom you don't know well? Find someone you can bring encouragement or service to in the body of Christ.

2. Who have been the main peacemakers in your life and what different tasks have they performed to bring you wholeness?

SCRIPTURE MEDITATION
*Matthew 18:21–35*

# Chapter Ten

POINTS FOR CONSIDERATION

1. Forgiving love is stronger than the power of violence, allowing us to go beyond the designation of enemy and to reach out for the other's common good.

2. You can claim your rights and show no mercy, but when your turn comes mercy may not be shown to you. All the important things in life—such as love and forgiveness—are two-way streets.

3. Turning the other cheek is one of the most difficult commands of Jesus, but every disciple must seek to do this with integrity, especially in an age of violence.

4. There is disagreement among Christians as to what amount of provocation is necessary to justify resorting to violence in self-defense. Some believe that force is justified in threatening situations, and they present pragmatic arguments based on safety and security. Others believe Jesus actually meant what He said about nonviolent love.

5. If you tend to resort to revenge, remember that God does not, or we would have no hope.


REFLECT AND ACT

1. When did you take the greatest risk in your life to love rather than be self-protective or retaliate? What did you gain and what did you lose?

2. Is turning the other cheek the right thing to do in every circumstance? What about when it comes to the protection of others?


SCRIPTURE MEDITATION
*Romans 12:20–21*

# Chapter Eleven

POINTS FOR CONSIDERATION

1. The goal of loving your neighbor as yourself is to make sure that your neighbor's needs are taken care of to the same degree that yours are.

2. We are not told to do absolutely everything that our neighbor requests because that may mean indifference to our neighbor's welfare. There are times when we need to lovingly set limits.

3. Love is not primarily feelings but actions and goes beyond emotions to express willing obedience and stubborn faithfulness, especially when it comes to restoring a broken relationship.

4. Agape love has aspects of benevolence, obedience, sacrifice, and justice. Forgiveness in its fullest sense expresses agape love or it falls short of the equal regard that heals.

5. The Golden Rule addresses such areas as equal listening, mutual appreciation, and reciprocal fairness toward others because it includes valuing the other's worth as much as your own.


REFLECT AND ACT

1. "Second mile" love means going far beyond common ideas of duty to make sure the needs of others are met. Who has best modeled this for you and why? How could you immediately implement this in your own life?

2. Have you ever loved a person without really liking them, or acted on that person's behalf without strong feelings? Why is this still love?


SCRIPTURE MEDITATION
*Matthew 5:41*

# Final Review

1. Find five descriptions of forgiveness that you may have not well understood before reading this book. What new insights do they give you?

2. Share with someone else at least one aspect of forgiveness that may give new insight and encourage that person to more effectively forgive or move toward reconciliation.

3. If love is the greatest commandment, what have you learned about the relationship between love and forgiveness as you encounter both God and your neighbor?

4. Out of all the barriers to forgiveness found in this book, with which one do you most struggle and how can you overcome it from the insights contained here?

5. Sometimes a relationship is restored after forgiveness, but the lingering pain stunts new growth. What action can you take now to improve one of those relationships?

6. As a result of your conclusions, write a one-page letter of commitment to improvement in the area of forgiveness as you continue on your Christian journey.

MORE SCRIPTURES FOR MEDITATION
*Luke 4:18–19; John 15:13; Luke 17:3–4; Matthew 5:39;*
*1 Peter 2:23–24; Proverbs 16:32; Romans 3:19; Luke 13:5;*
*Matthew 7:12; Romans 12:4–5; James 1:19–20*

Moody Press, a ministry of Moody Bible Institute,
is designed for education, evangelization, and edification.
If we may assist you in knowing more about Christ
and the Christian life, please write us without obligation:
Moody Press, c/o MLM, Chicago, Illinois 60610.